PHILADELPHIA LIGHT

Deep Space Astro-photographers record the past. They capture light that has taken hundreds, thousands, and millions of light years to reach the earth. The photographs of the "Philadelphia Light" portfolio is similar - captured in the period 1973 – 1978 (dates are approximate) the negatives were stored and hidden for many years. Now, the light that formed the images on the silver-halide based negatives reached earth in 2019 in the form of a book.

The photographs, taken in Philadelphia primarily in the "center city" area, always made with a select set of characteristics: bright sunlight and large areas of negative space, subjects captured in between conscious thoughts, dreamlike states, and a social narrative of the society that inhabited the walls of the city. The camera was a Leica M3 using Tri-X film.

The photographs illustrate subjects where status, appearance, career, age, and class are irrelevant. The stark sunlight and camera capture reveals everyone is equal – all human in expression and desire. These images, like frames of a movie, merge into another dimension un-stuck in time.

One thought that science and astronomy teach us is the finite nature of the human species. From a relative time, perspective, we have only inhabited the earth for a micro-second, the universe for an inestimable slice, and the species will expire soon. The Sun becomes a red giant that engulfs the earth and solar system and then implodes to create a nebula of gas and dust that form new stars, planets, solar systems, and life. This finality should be driving us at every moment to evolve beyond "isms" invented by human folly to achieve harmony in everything we do.

Turn your face to the Sun, and the shadows fall behind you.

The entire portfolio: https://www.unKOwnphotographer.com

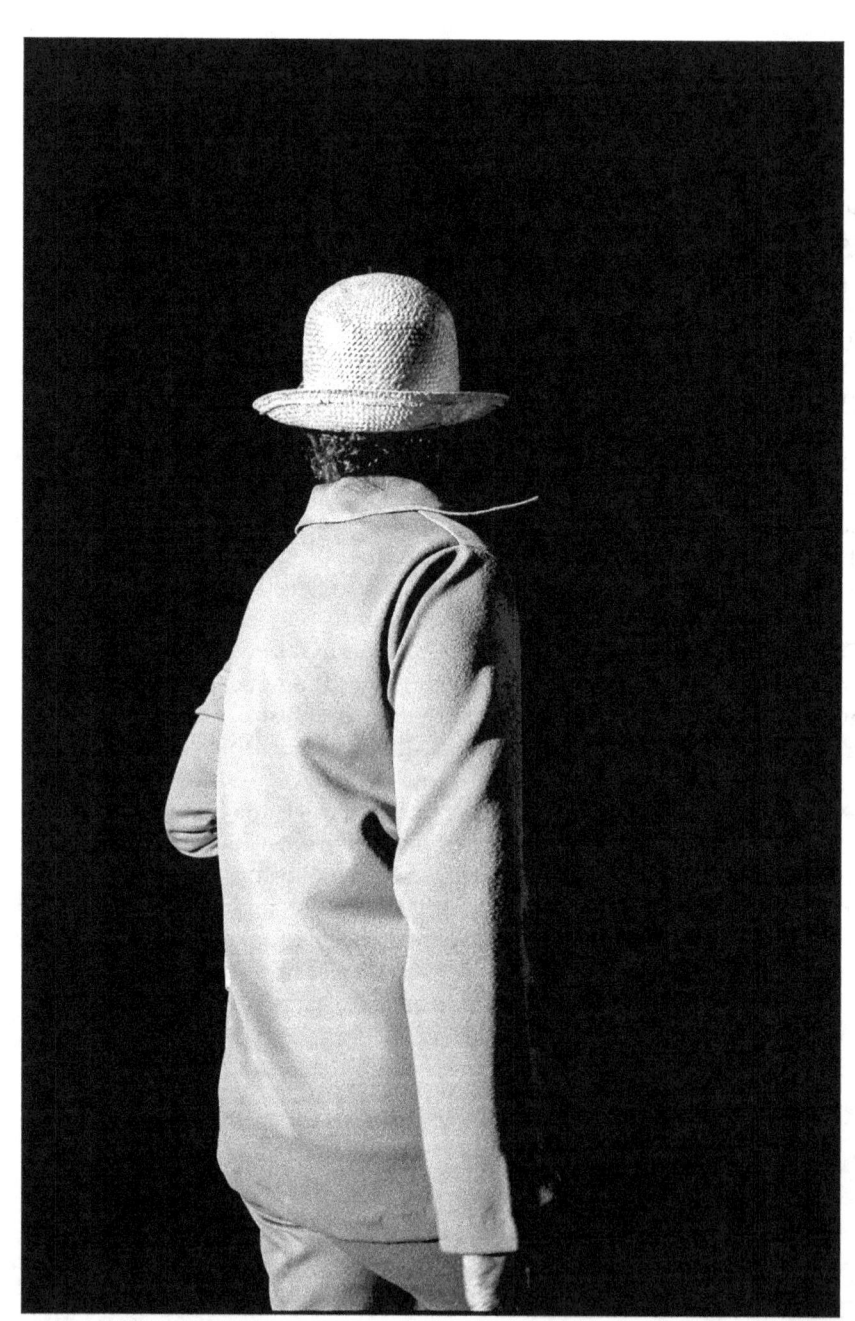

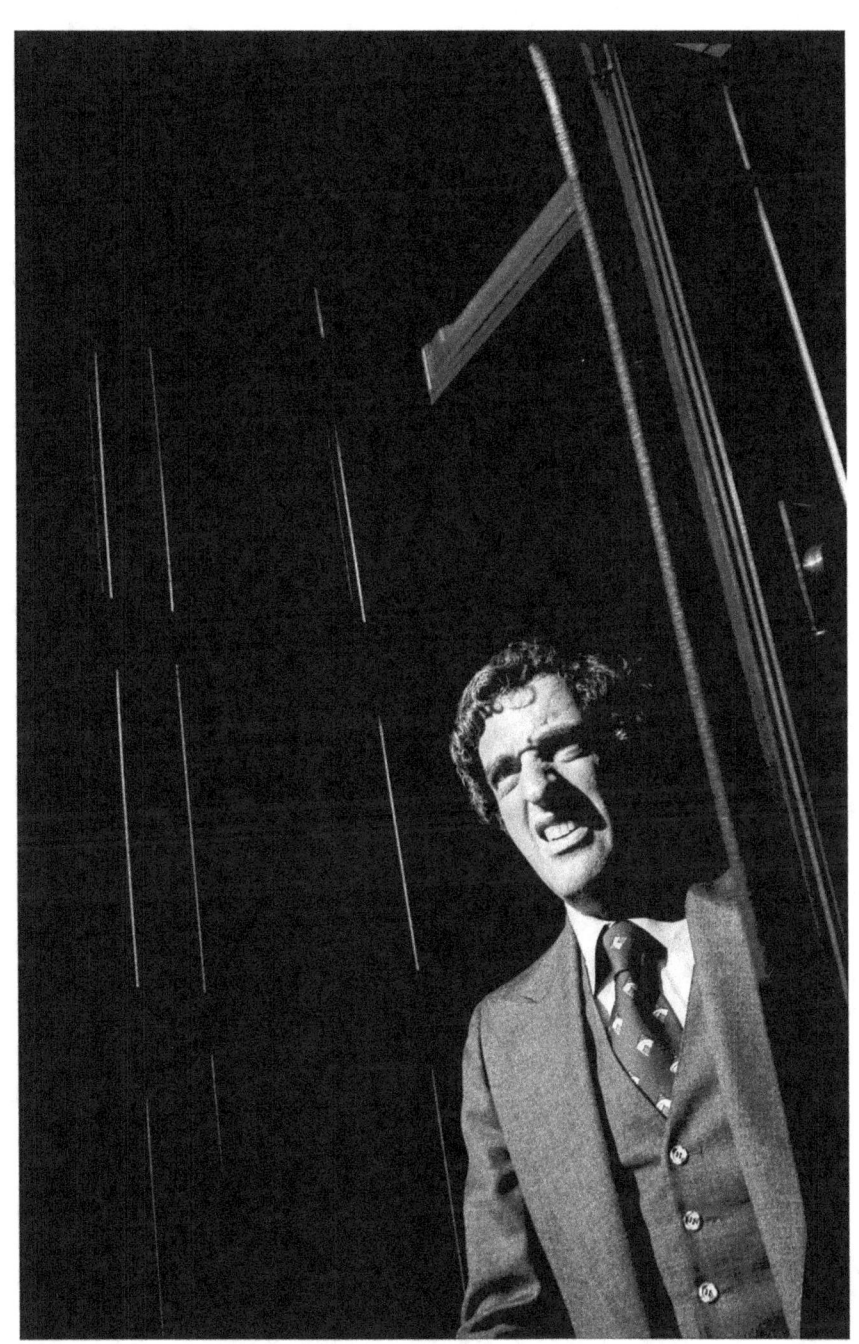

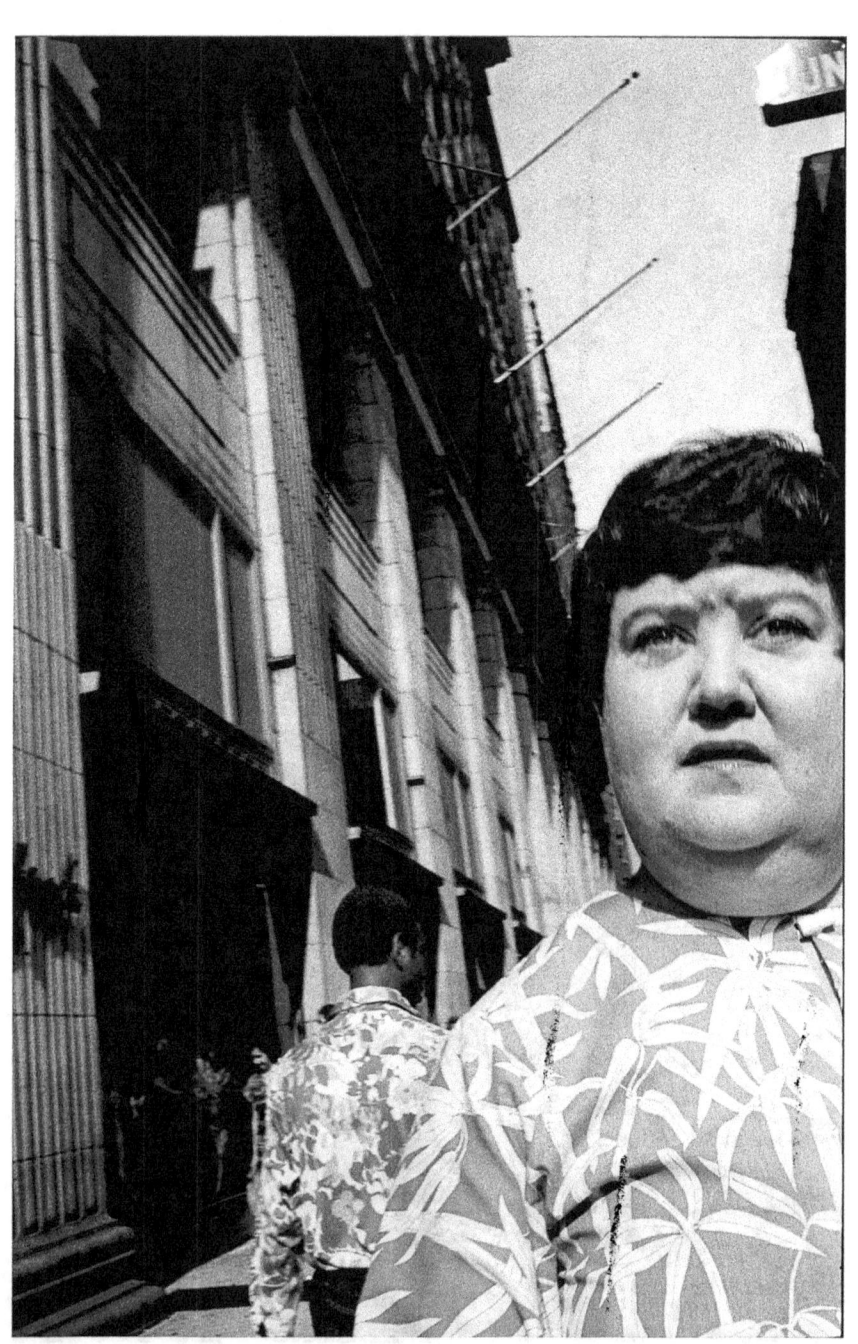

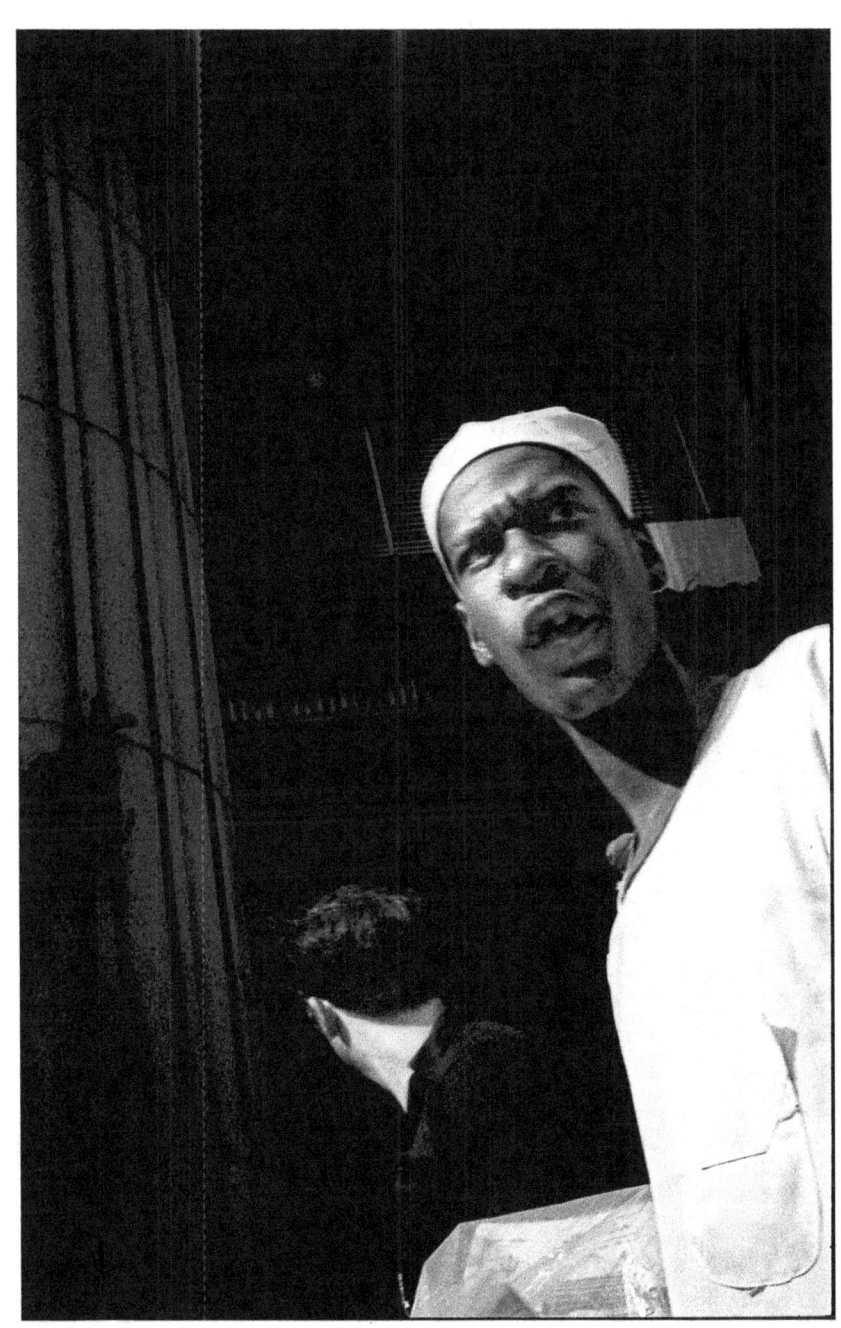

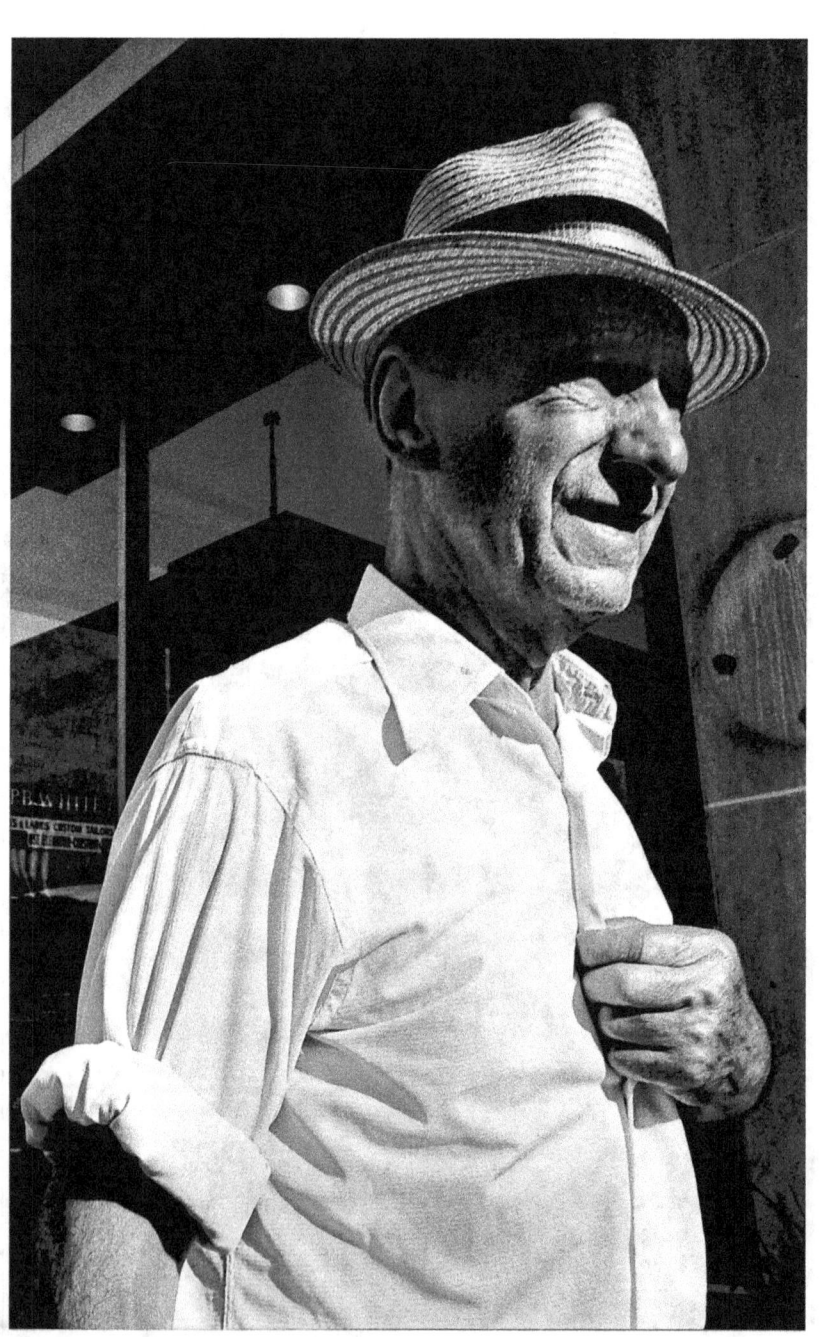

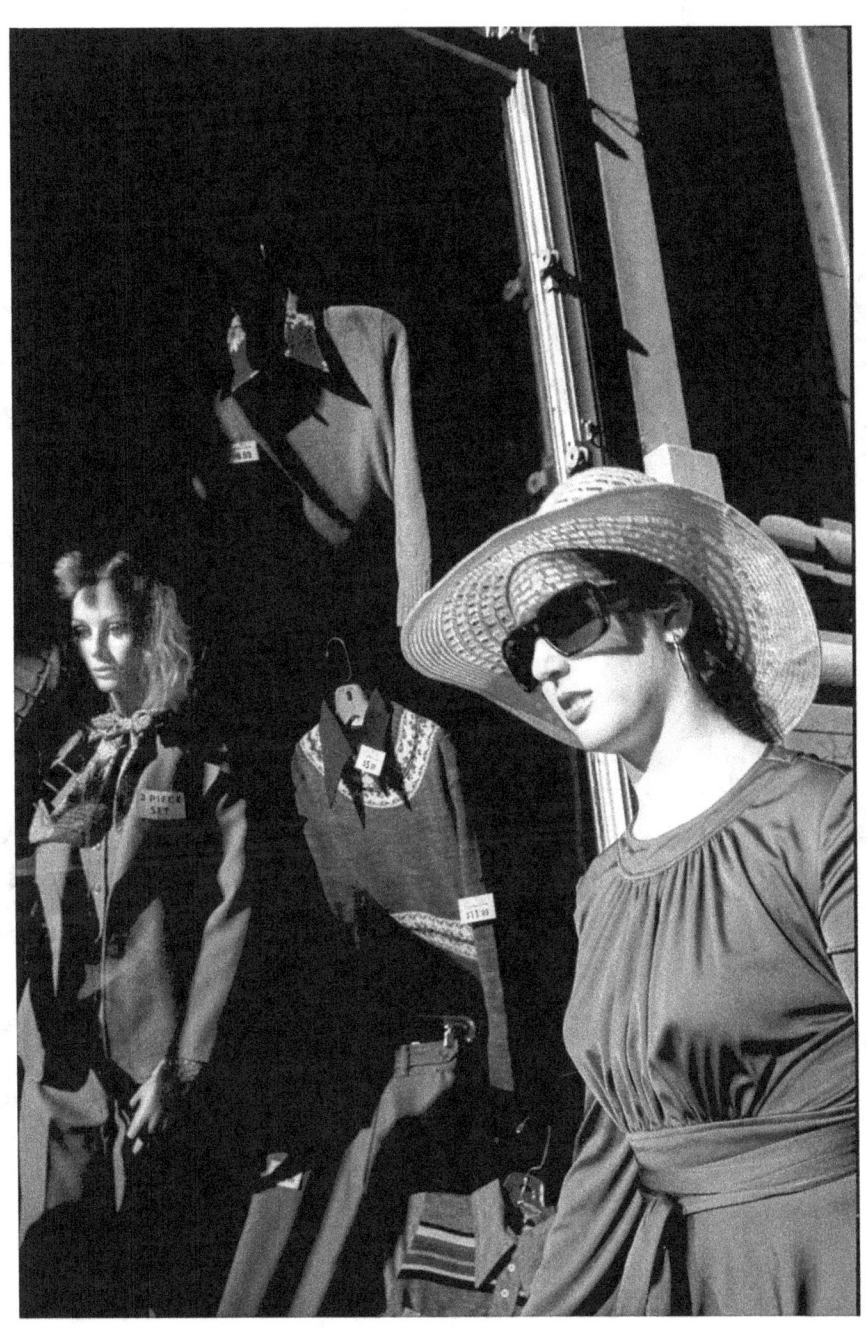

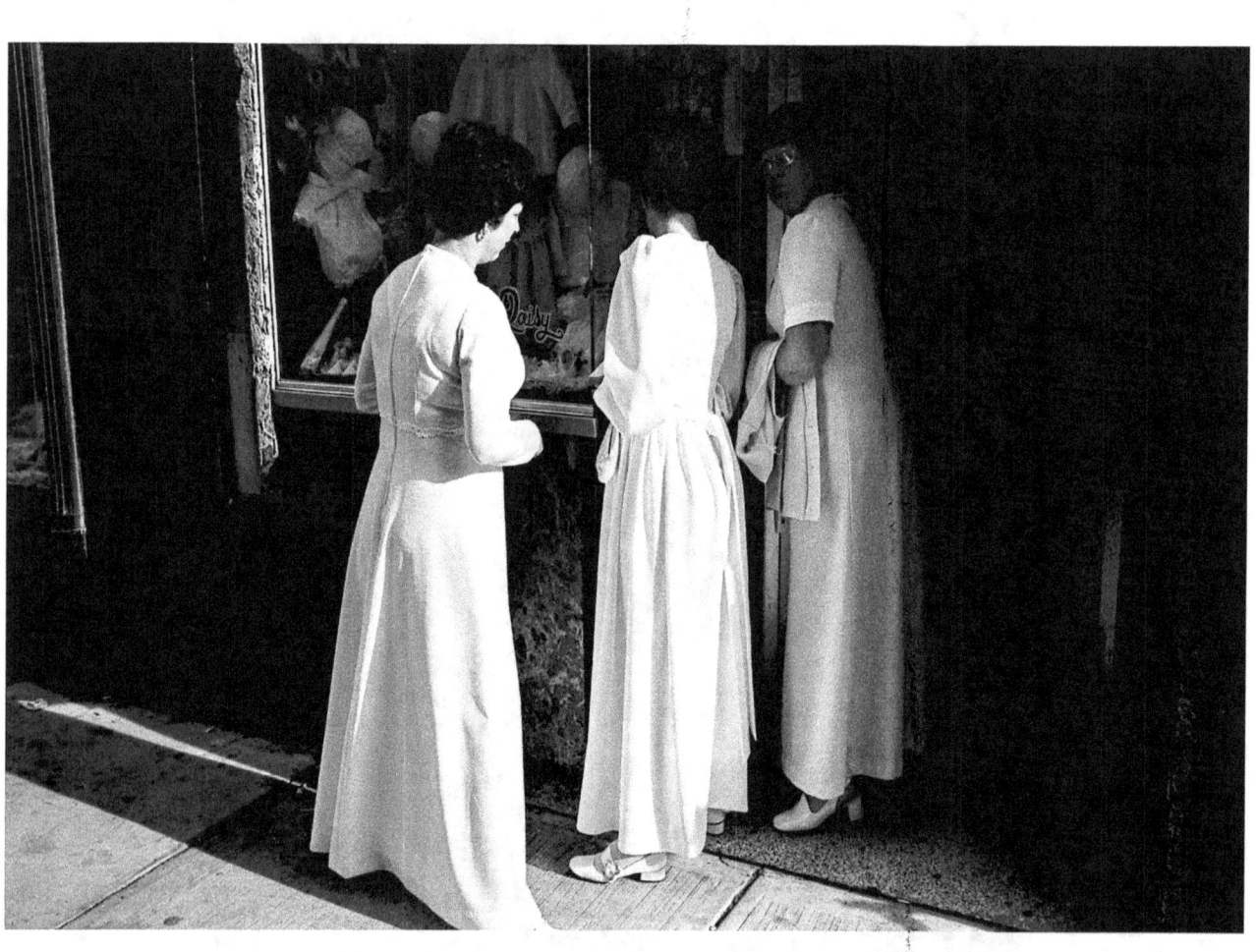

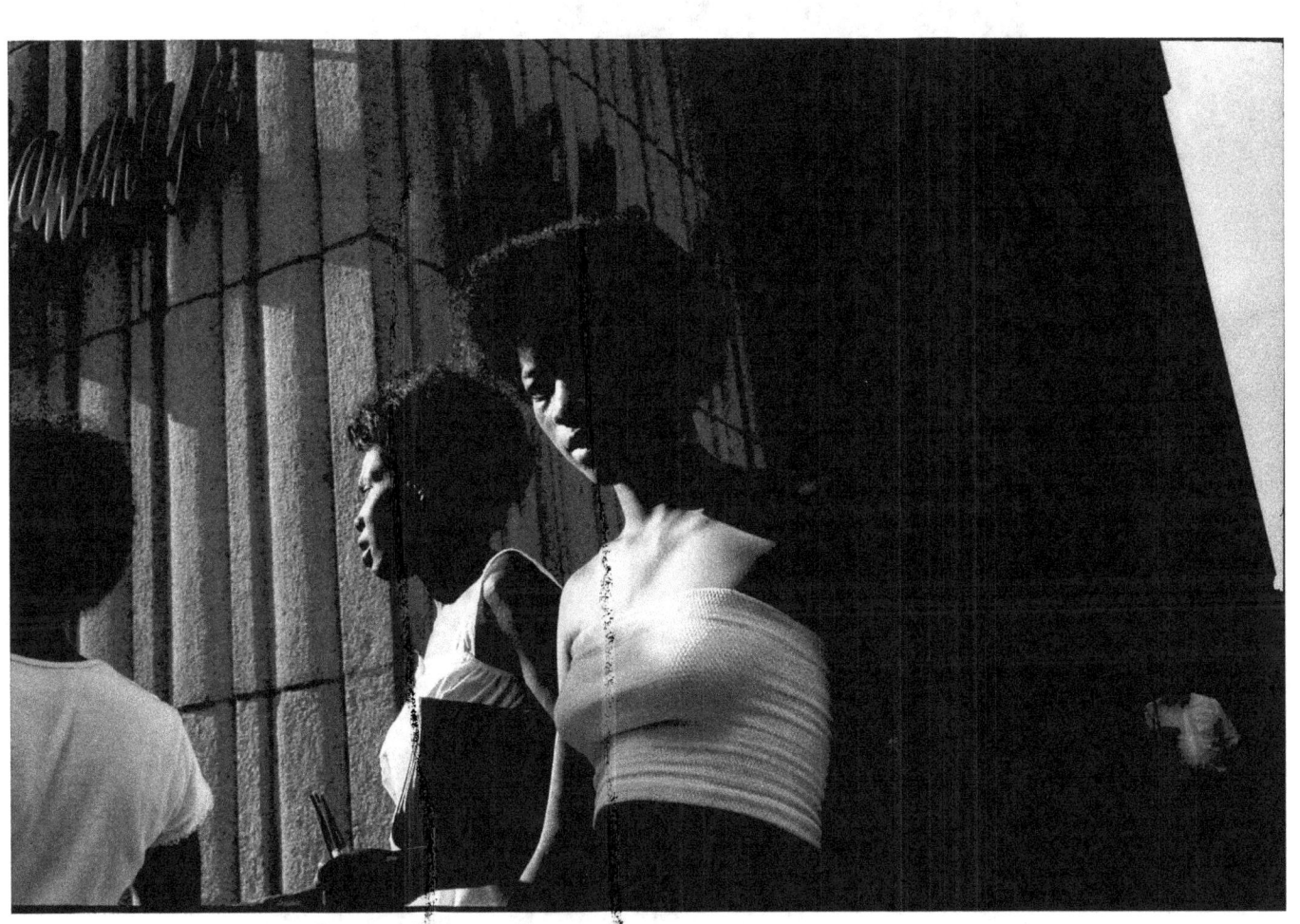

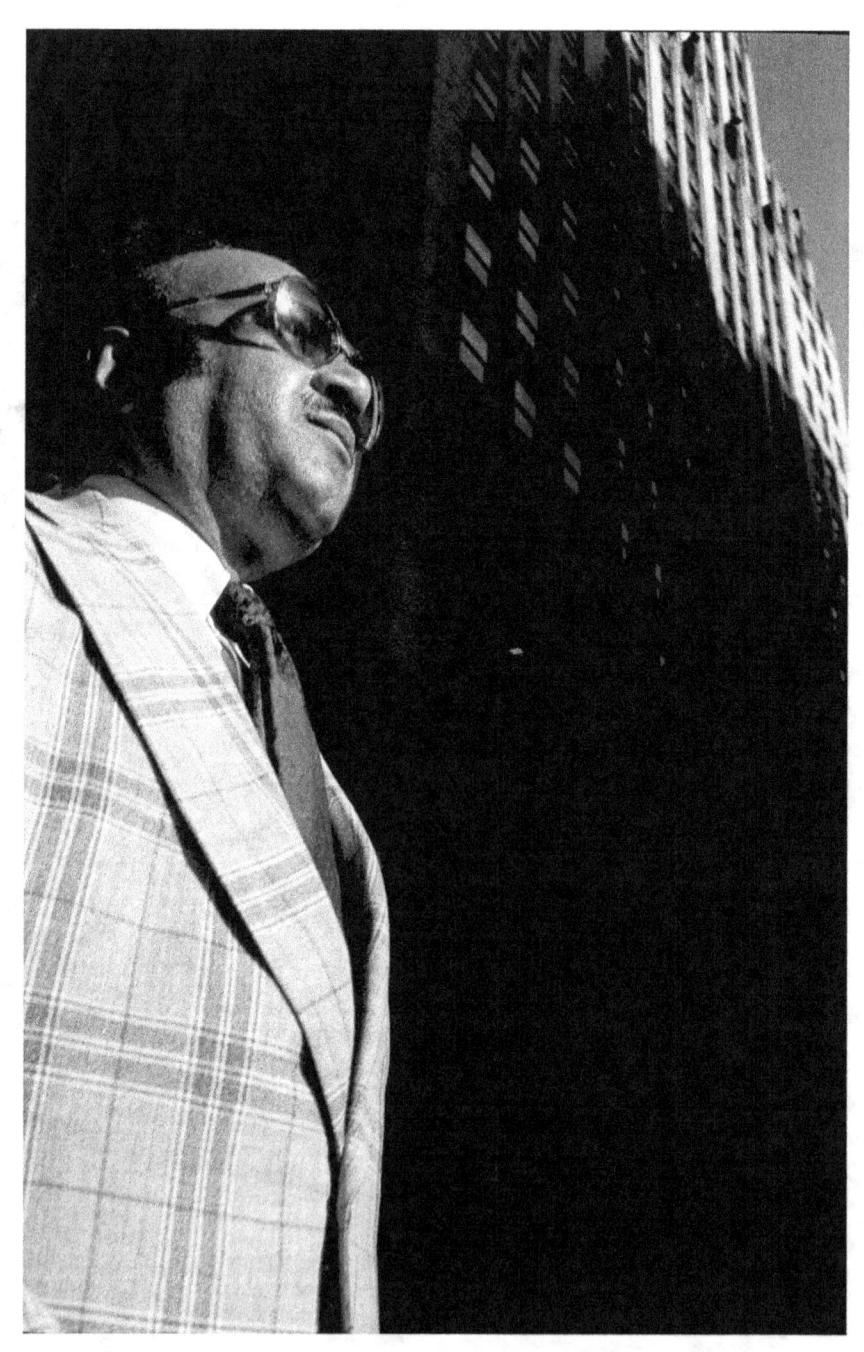

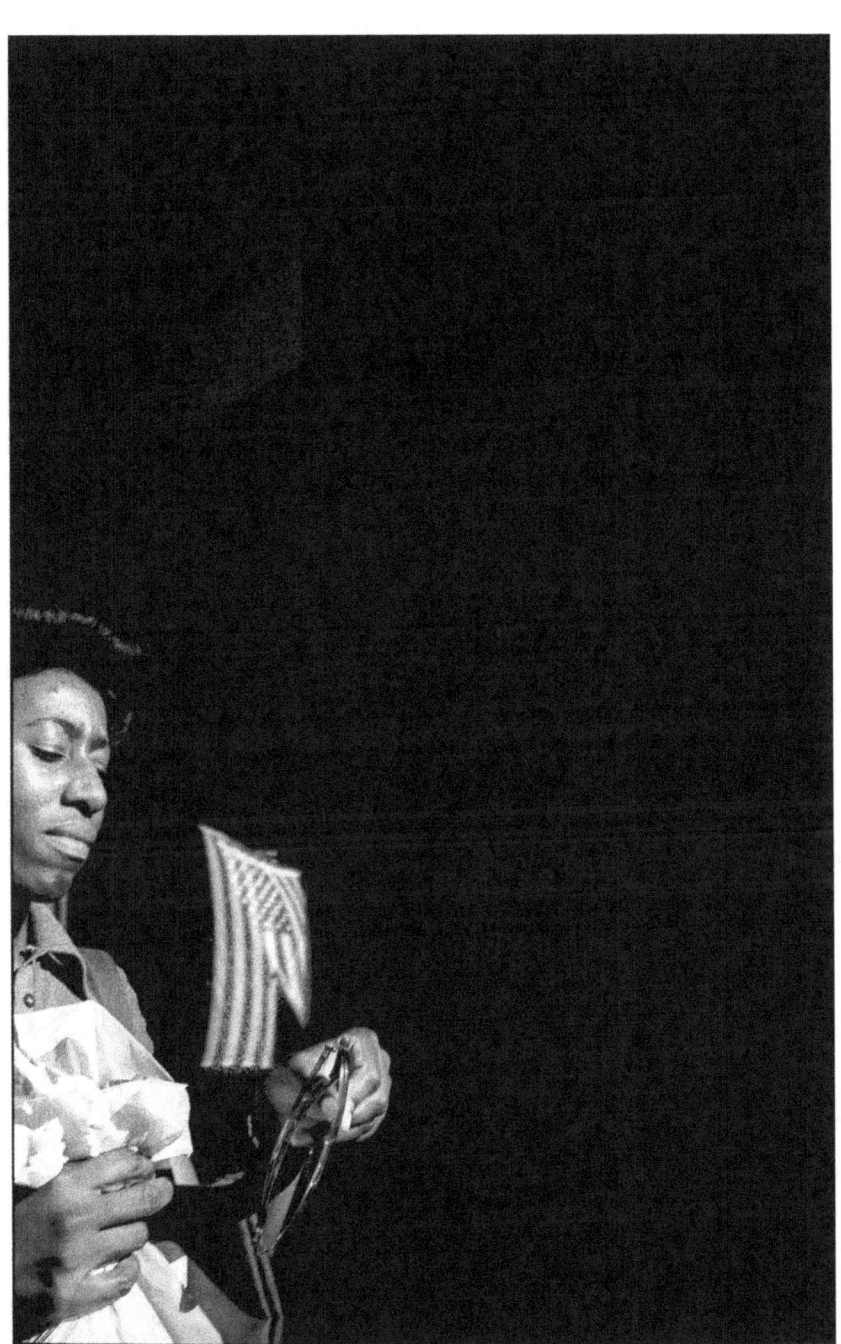

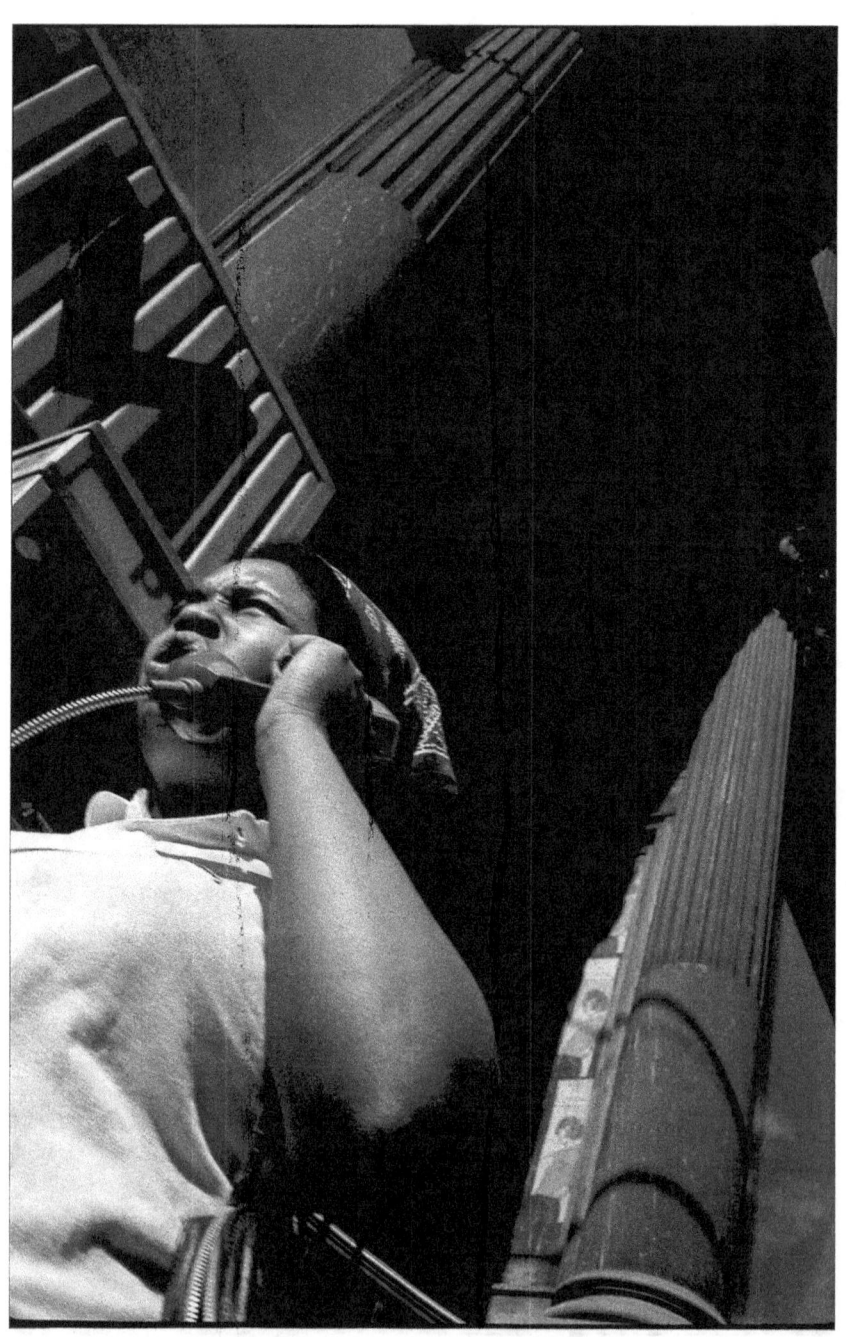

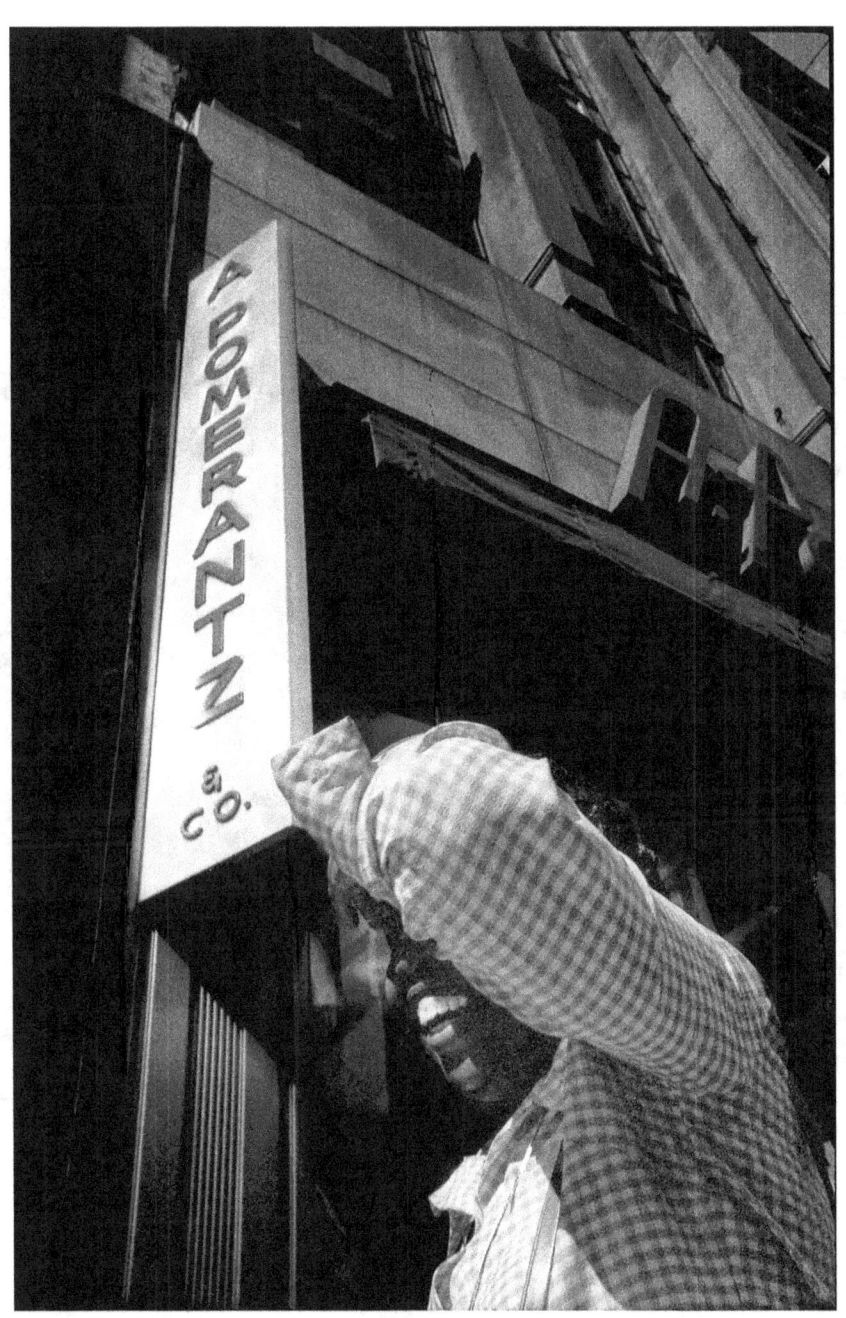

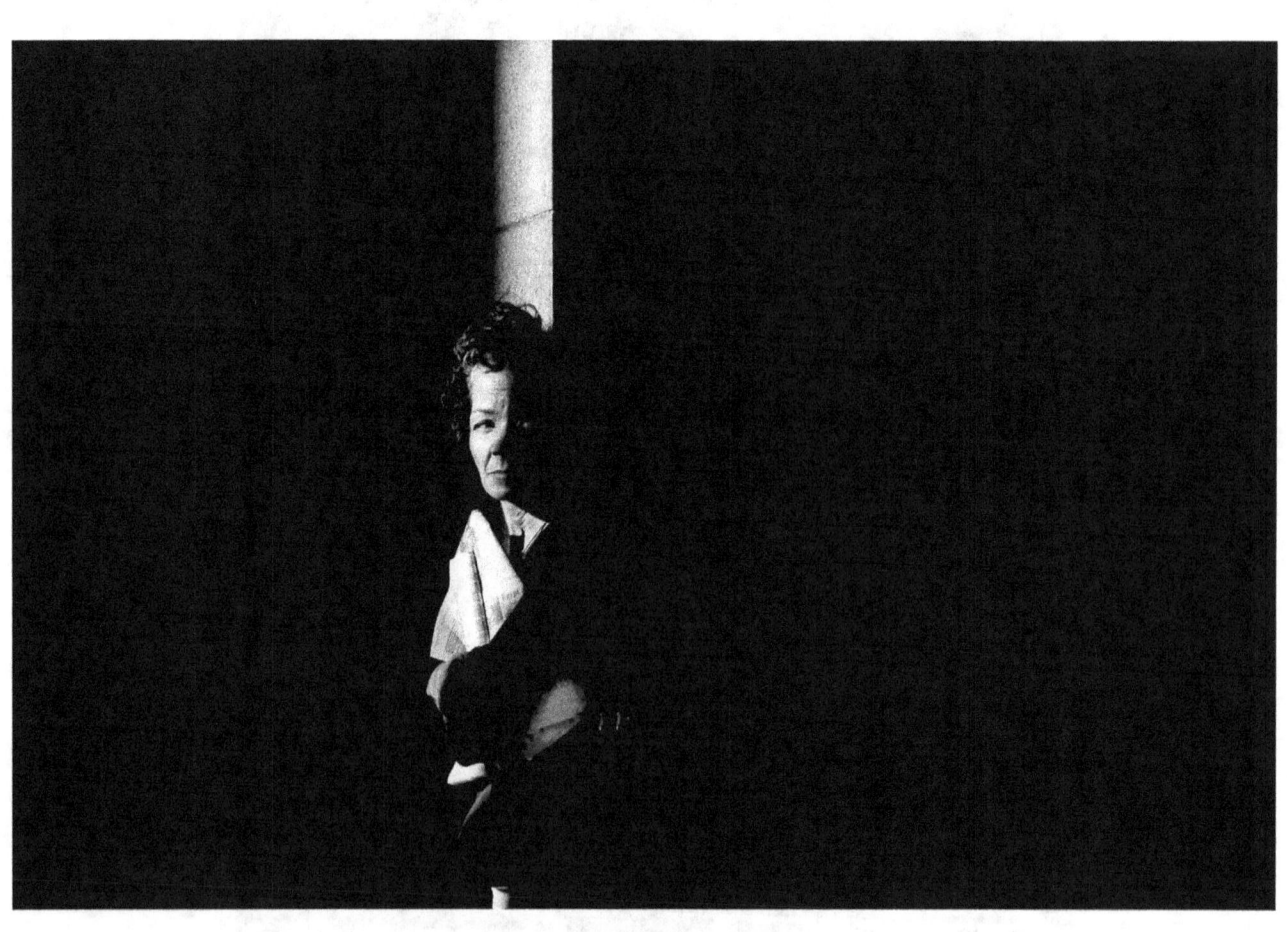

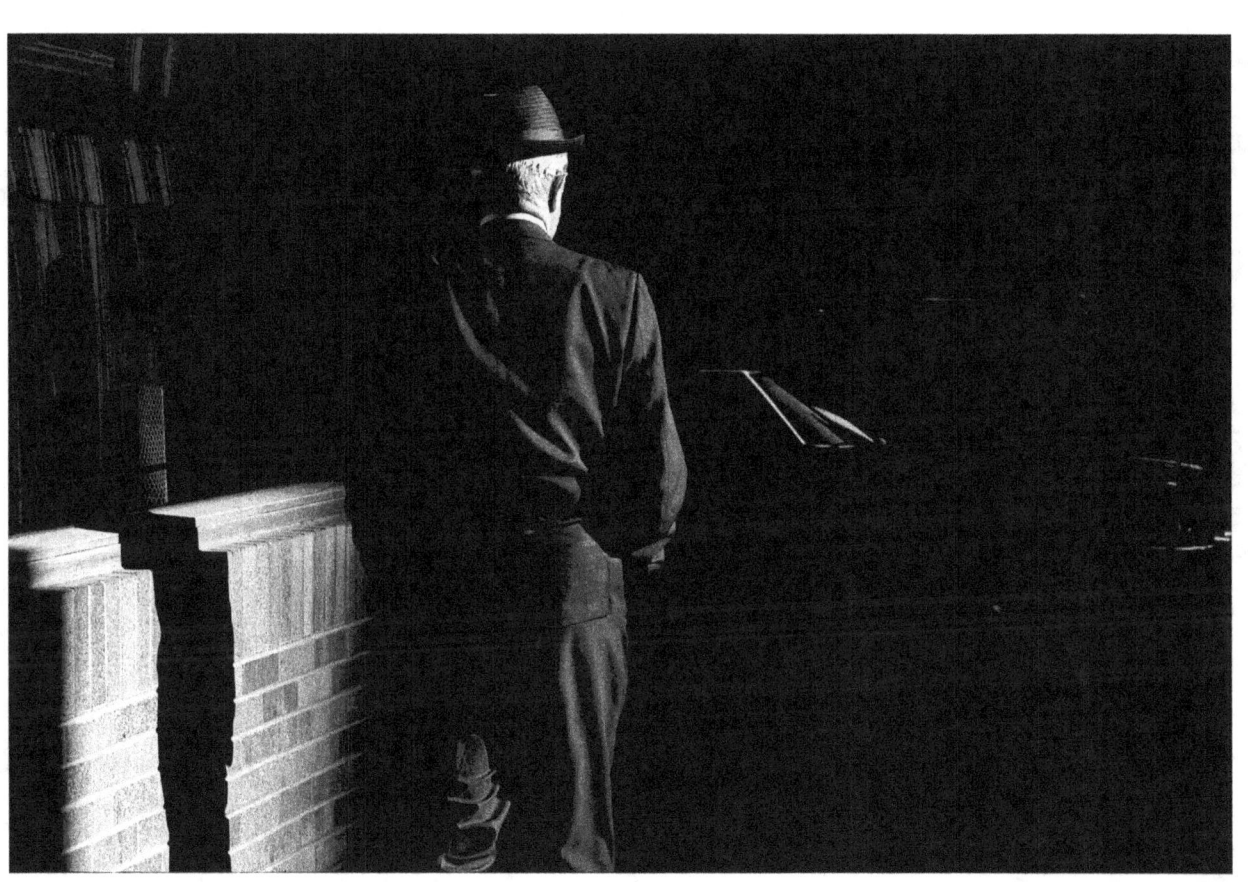

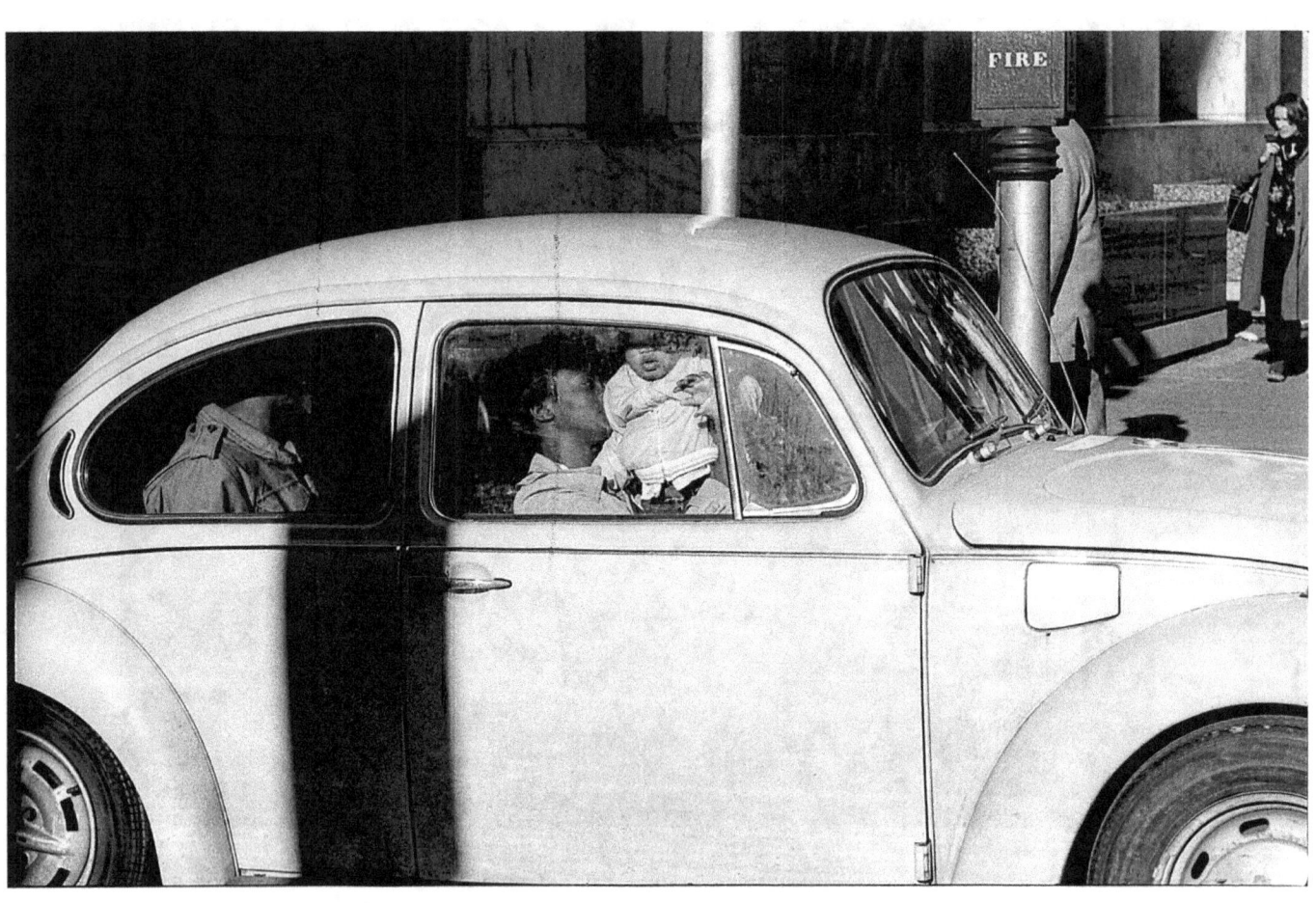

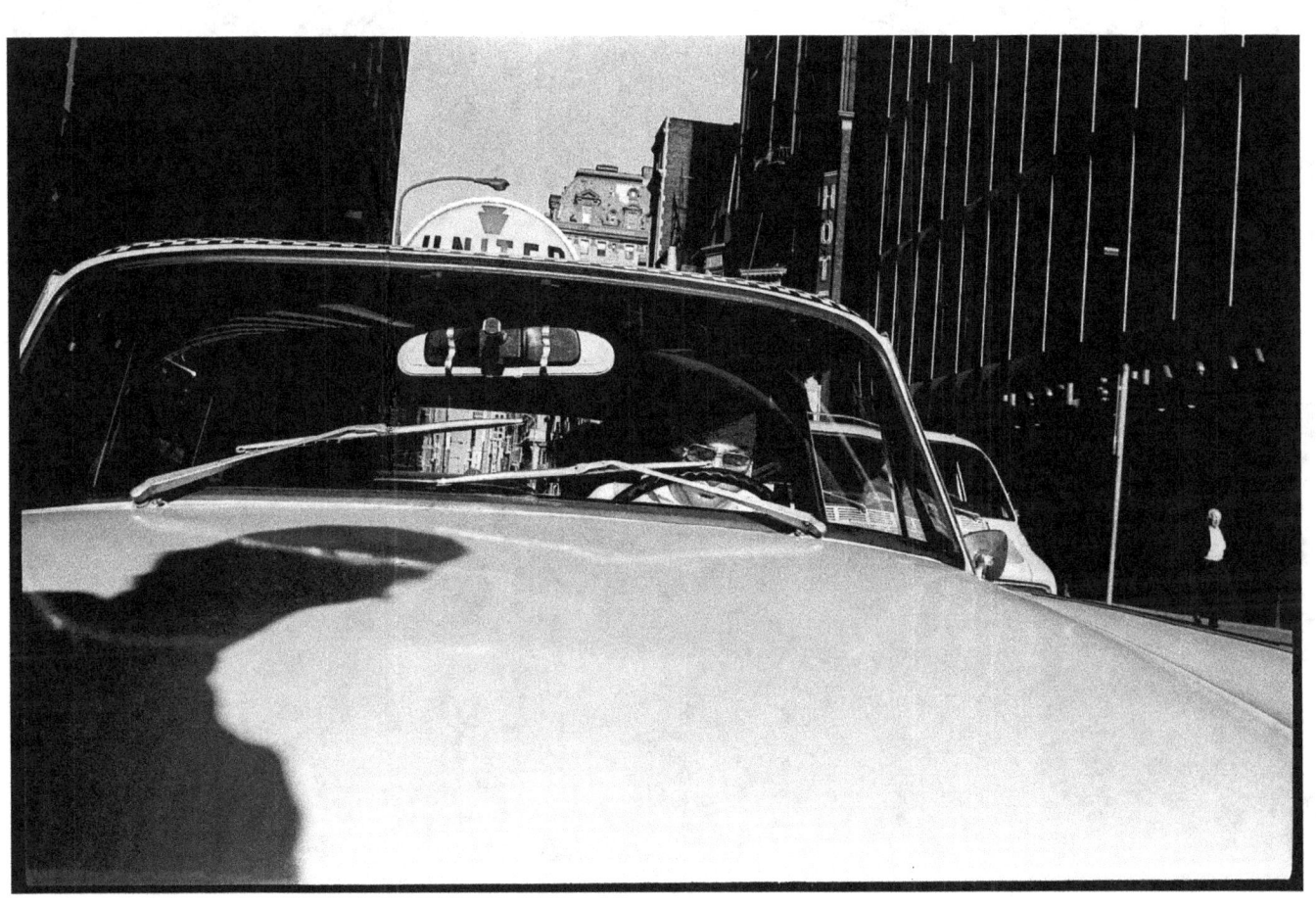

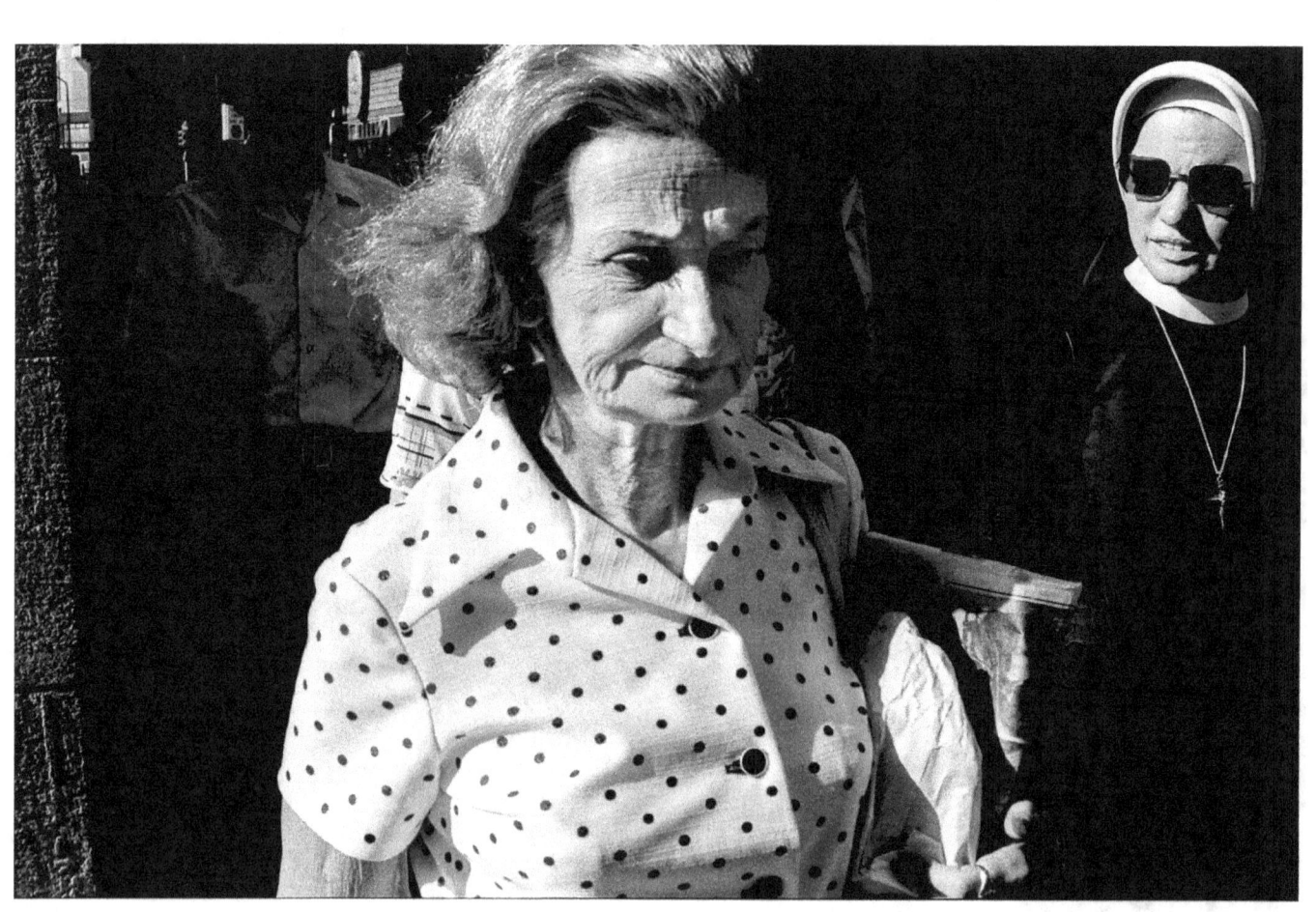

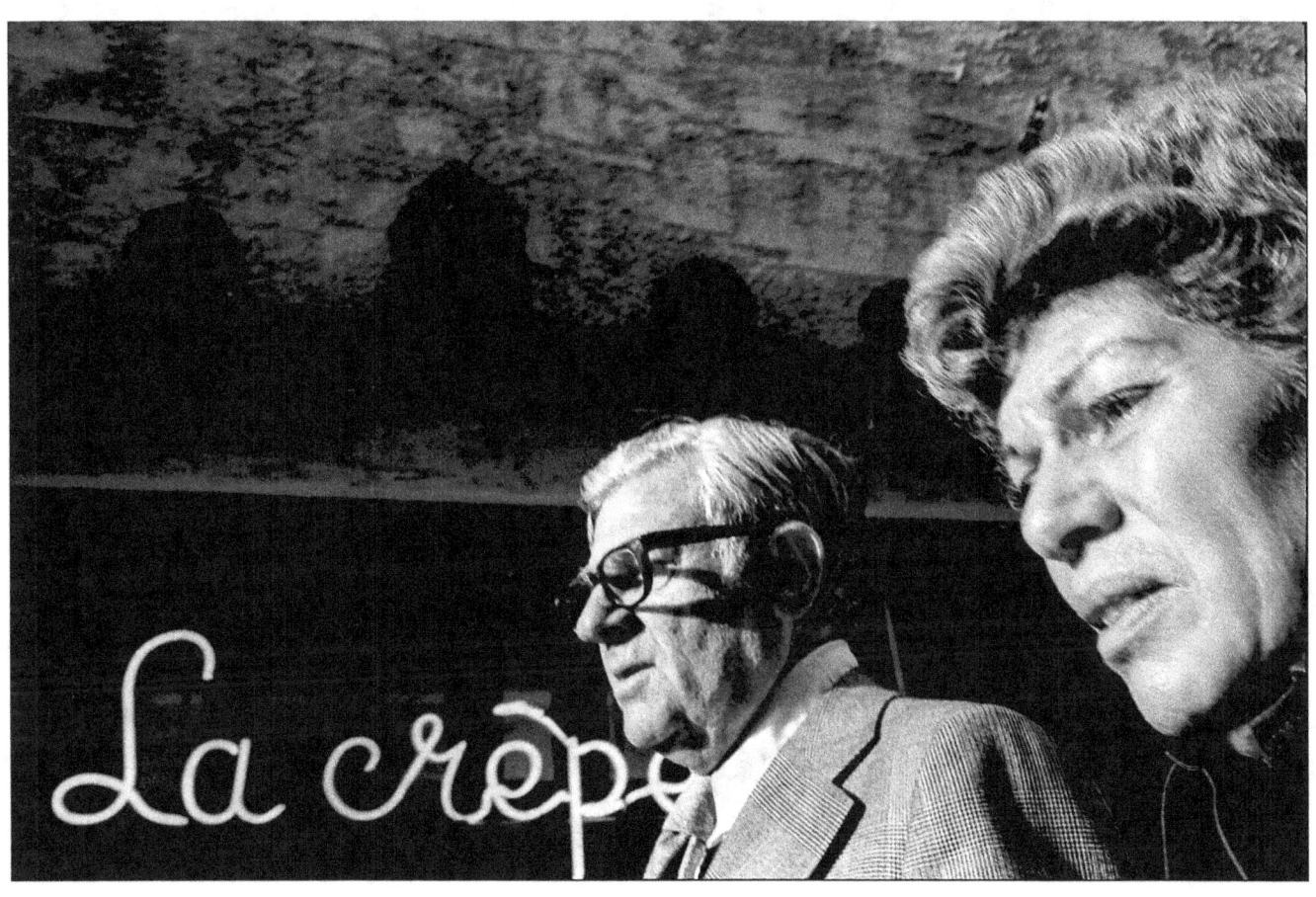

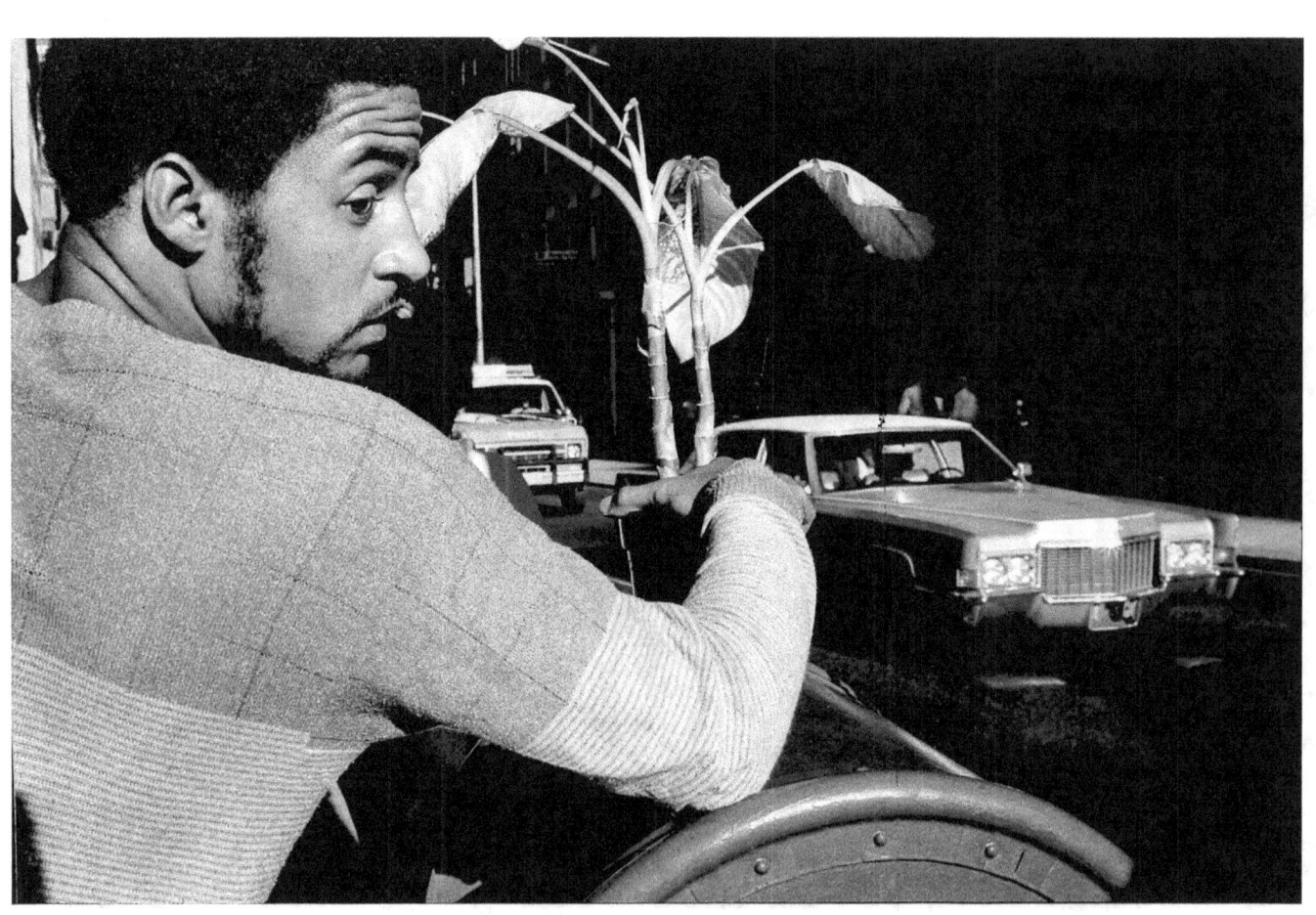

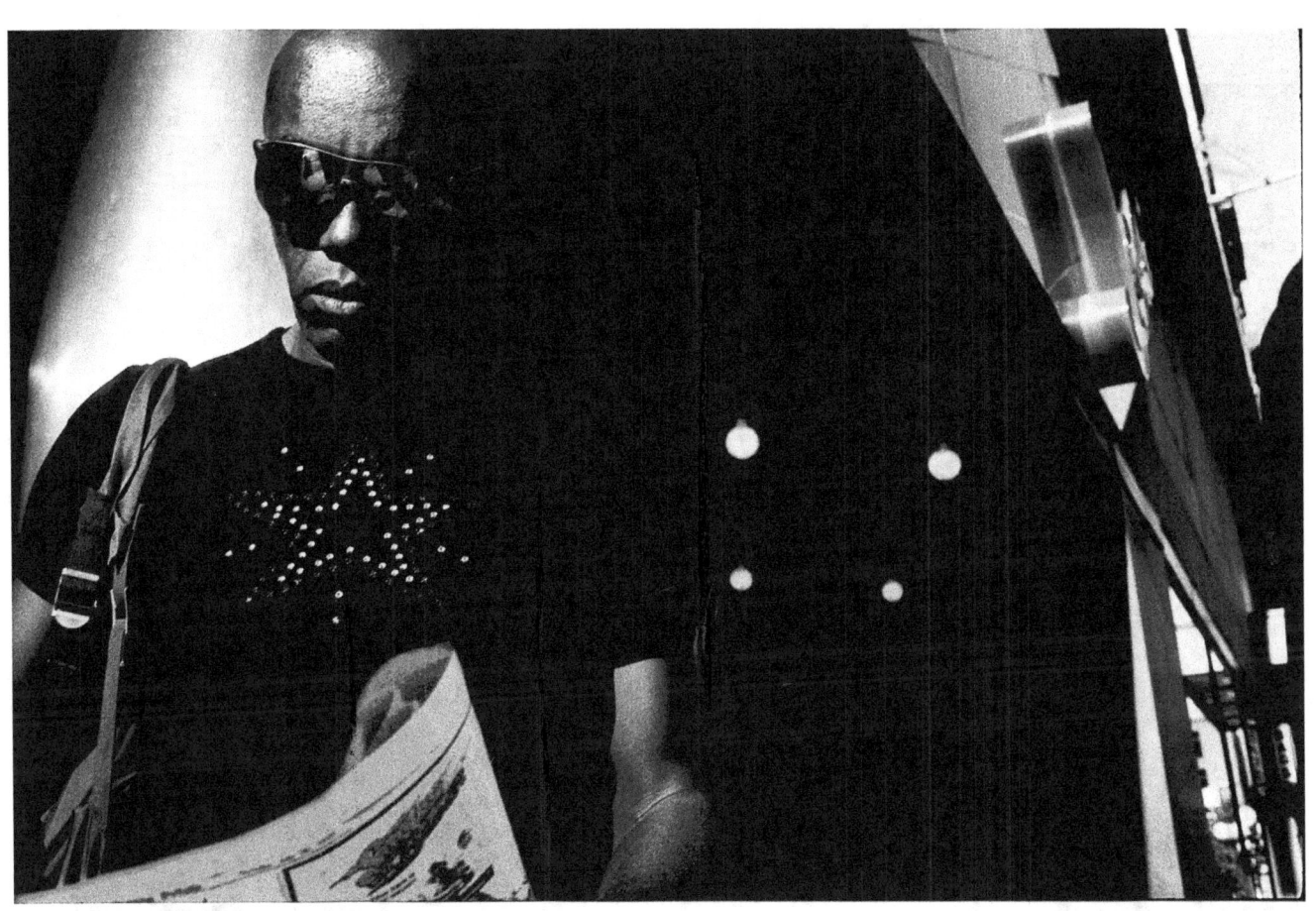

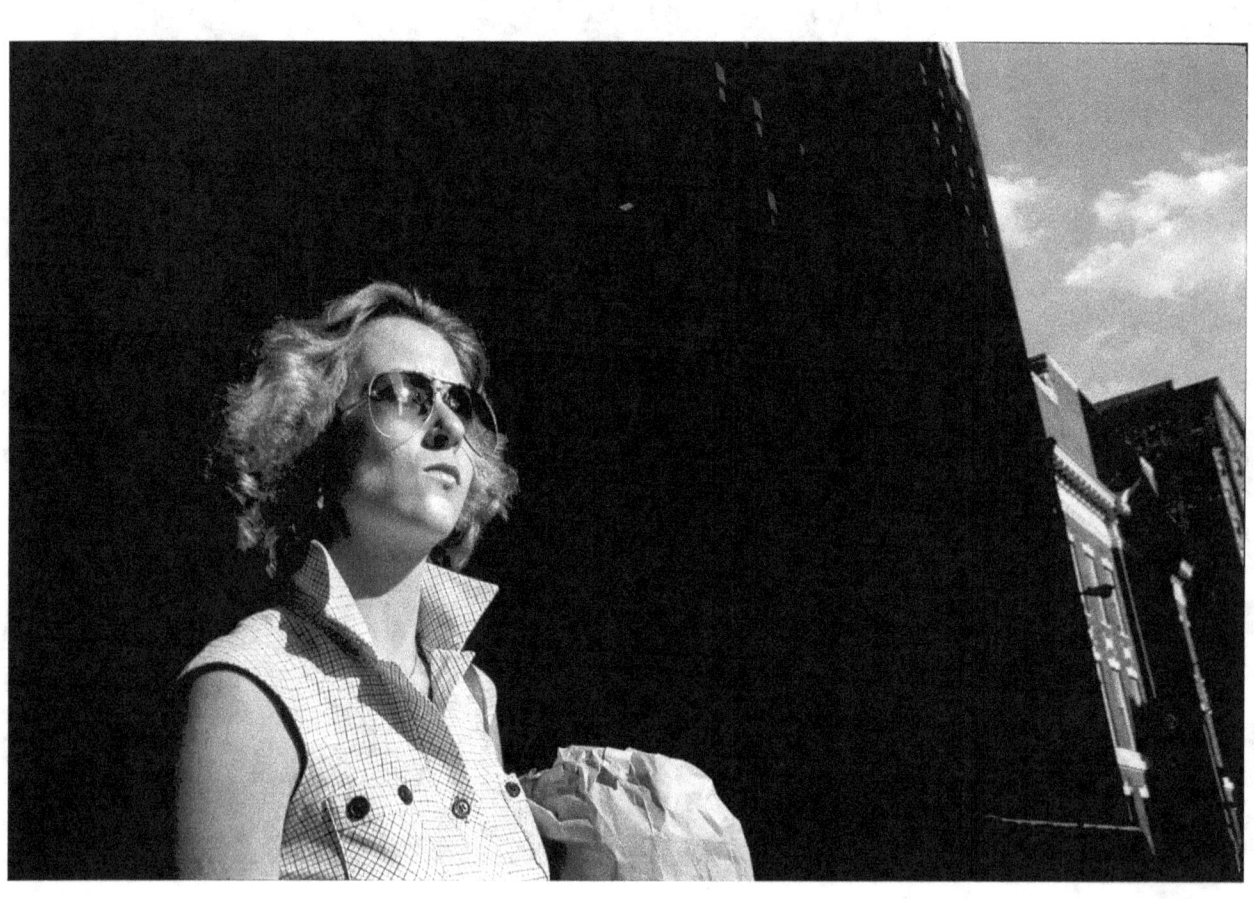

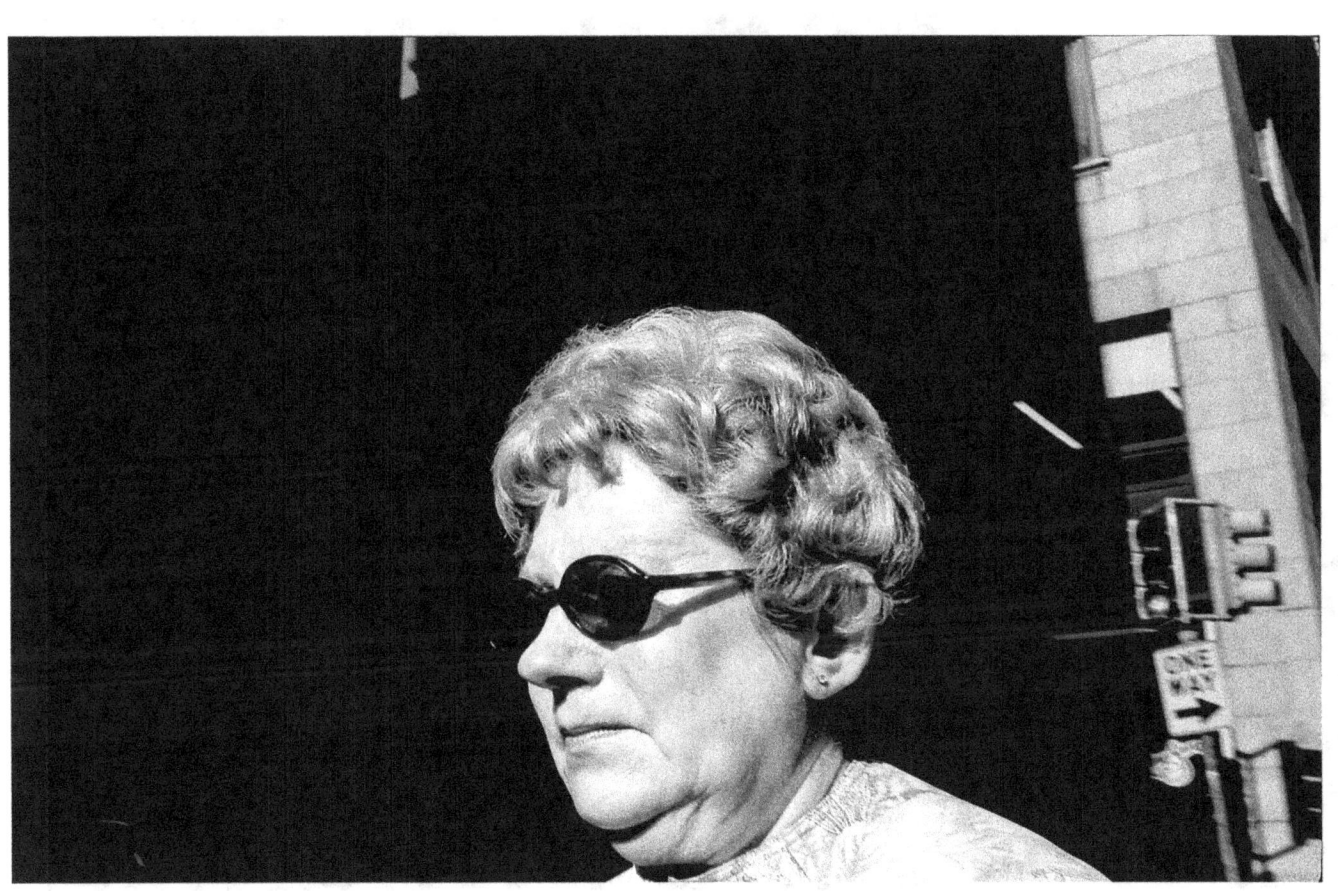

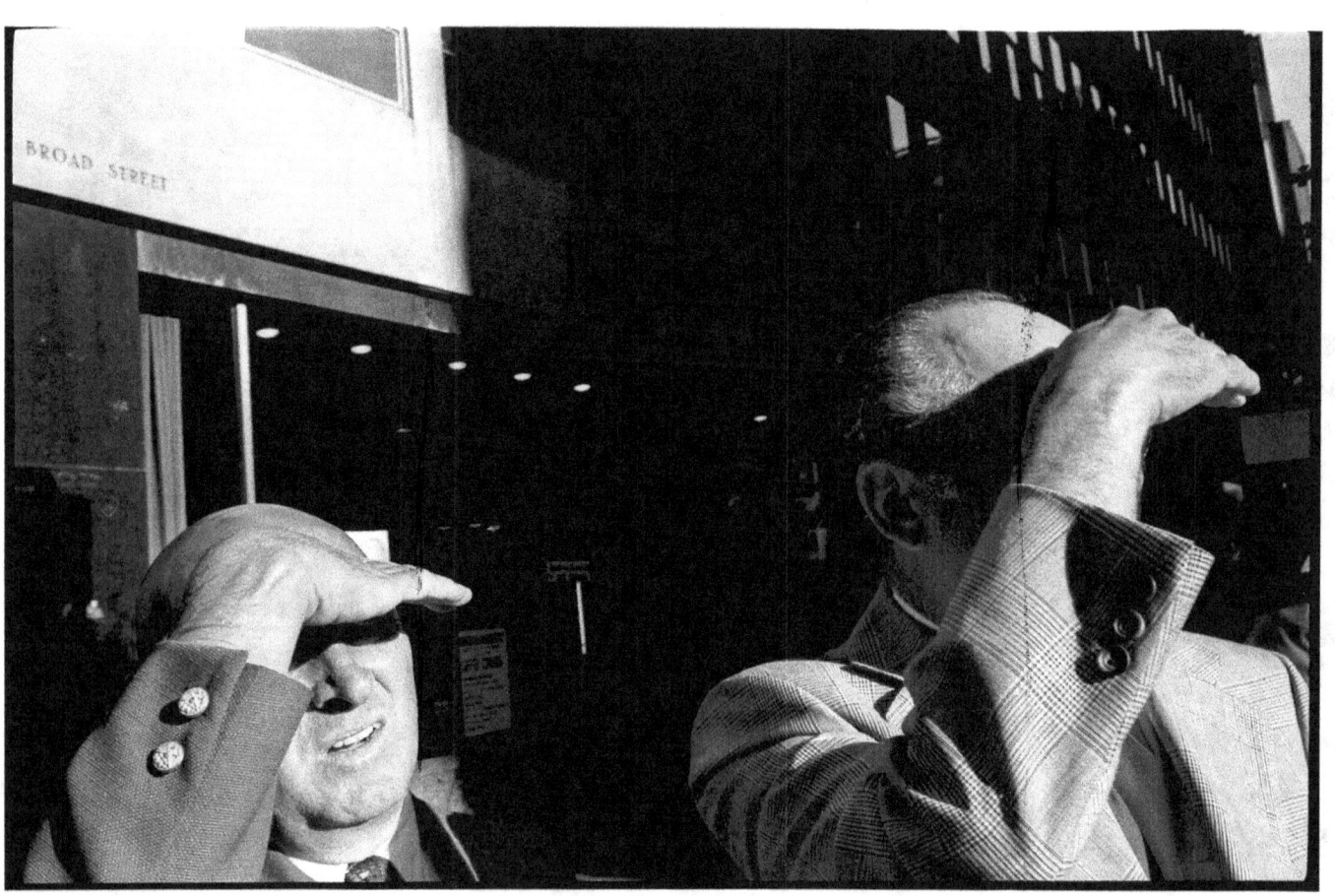

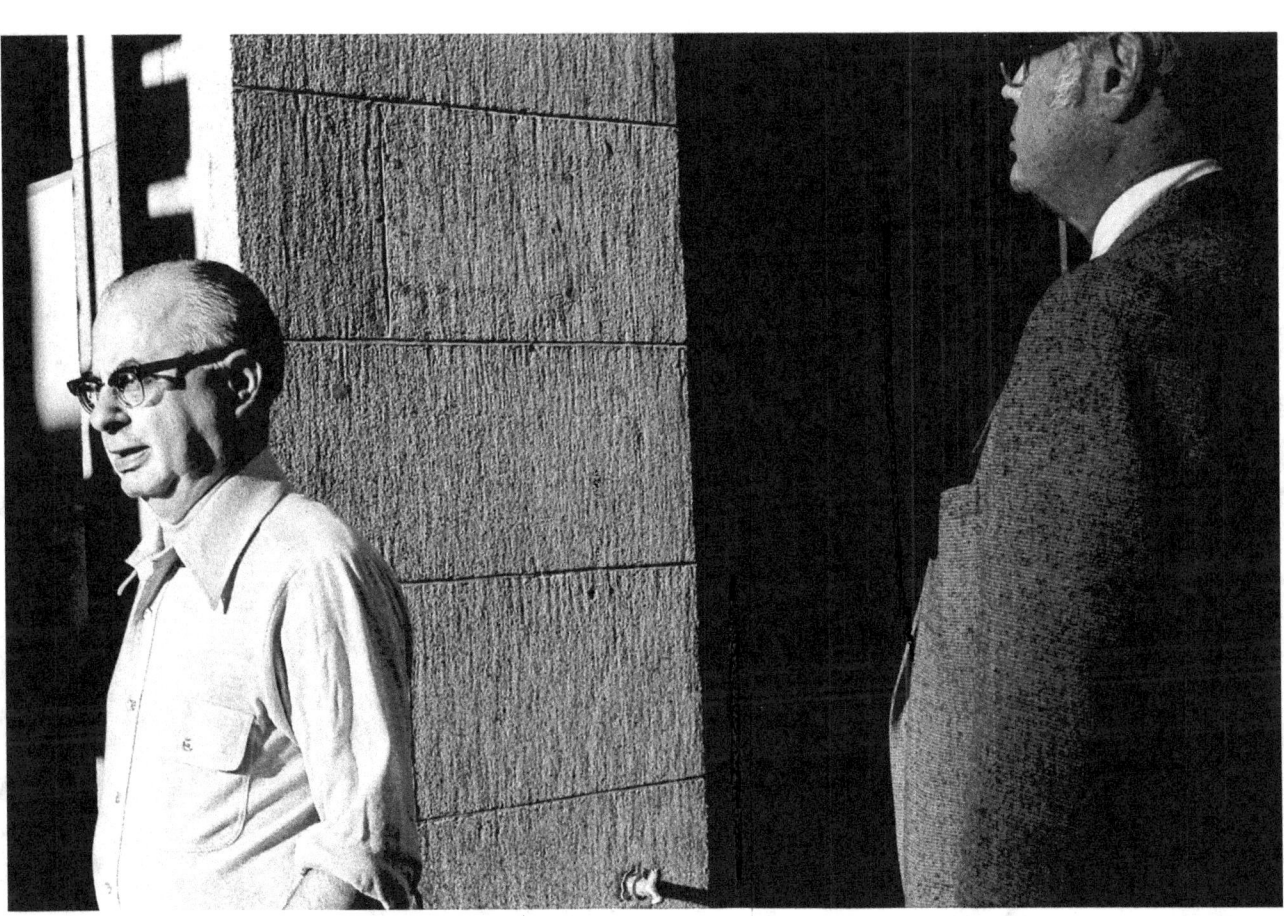

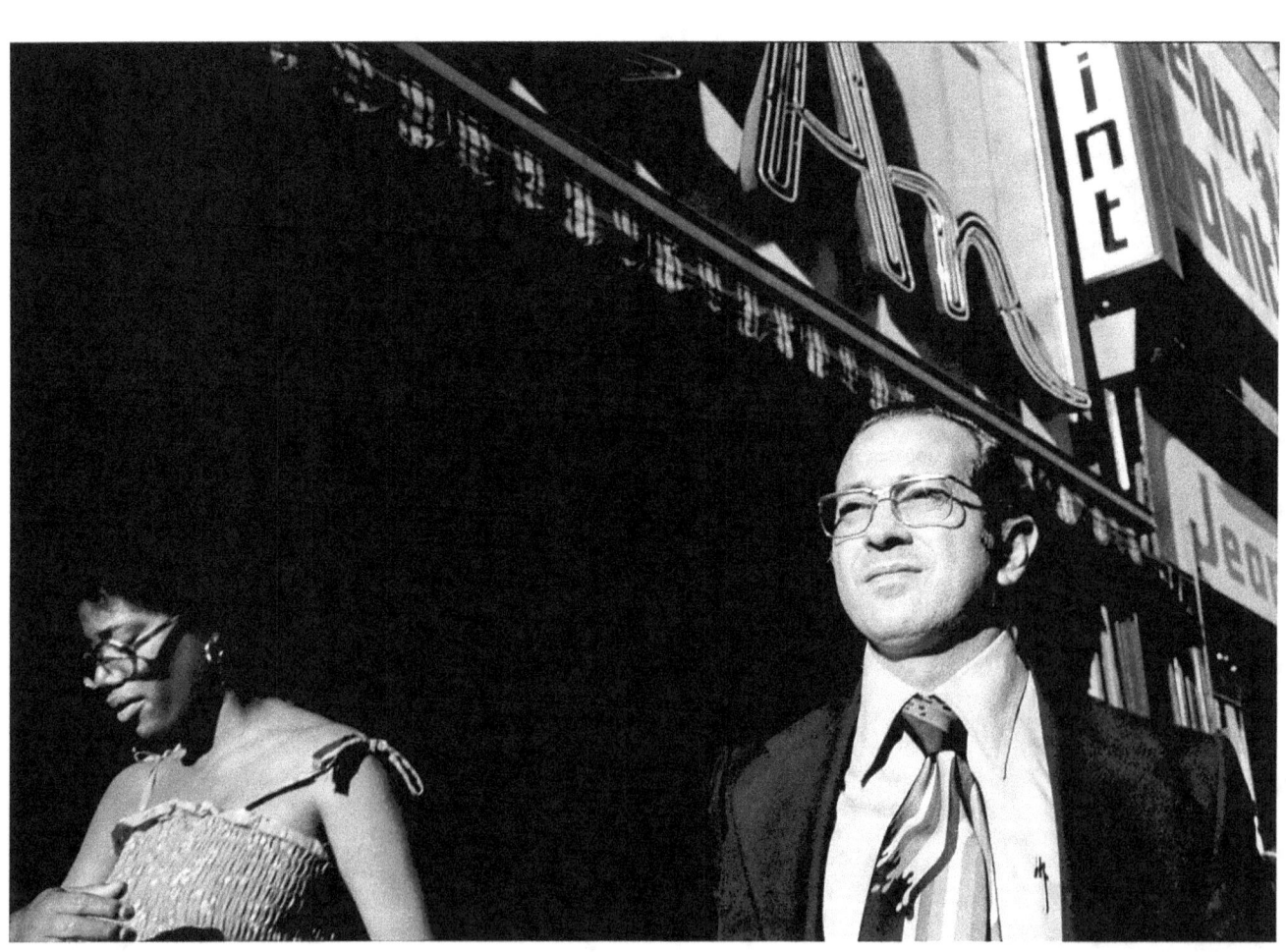

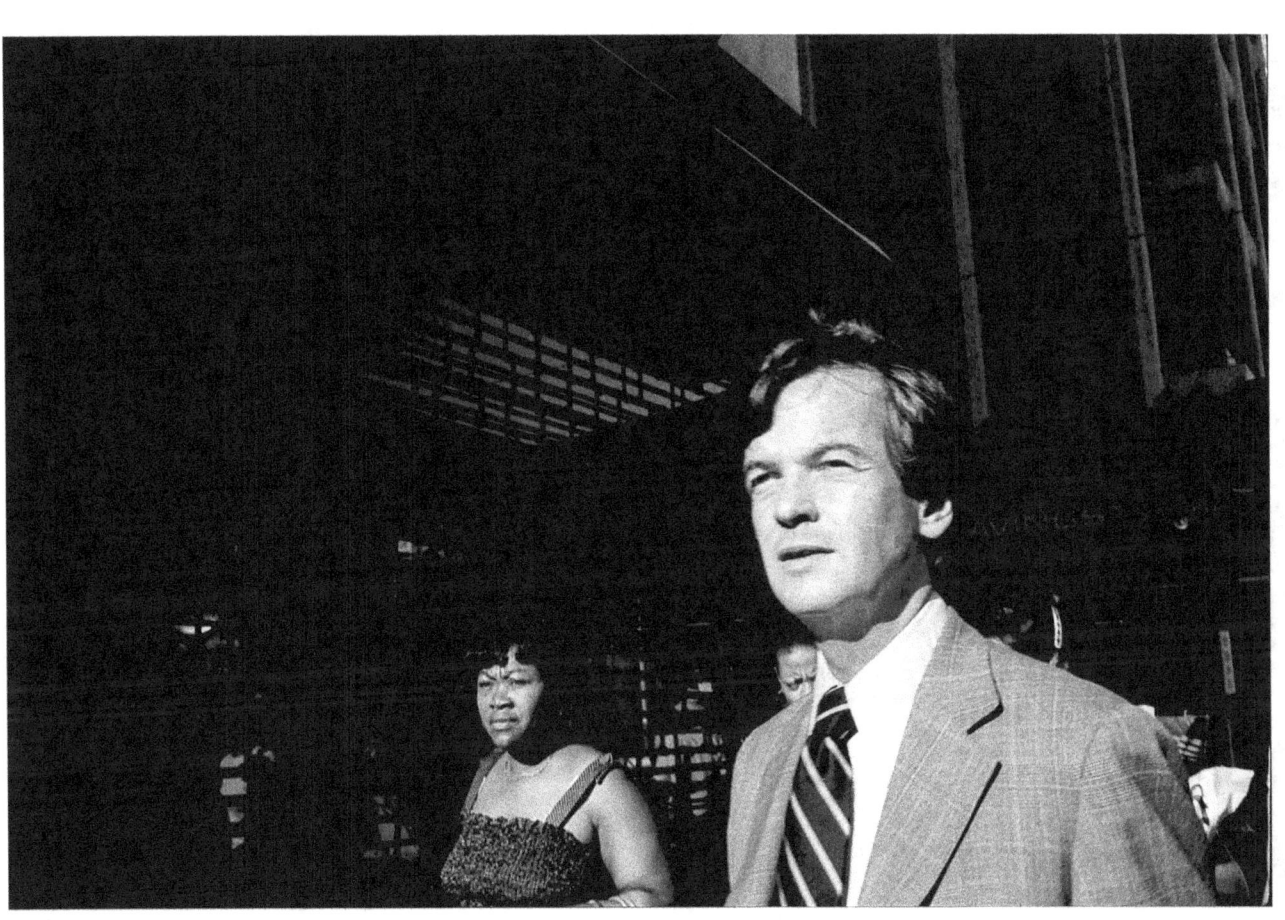

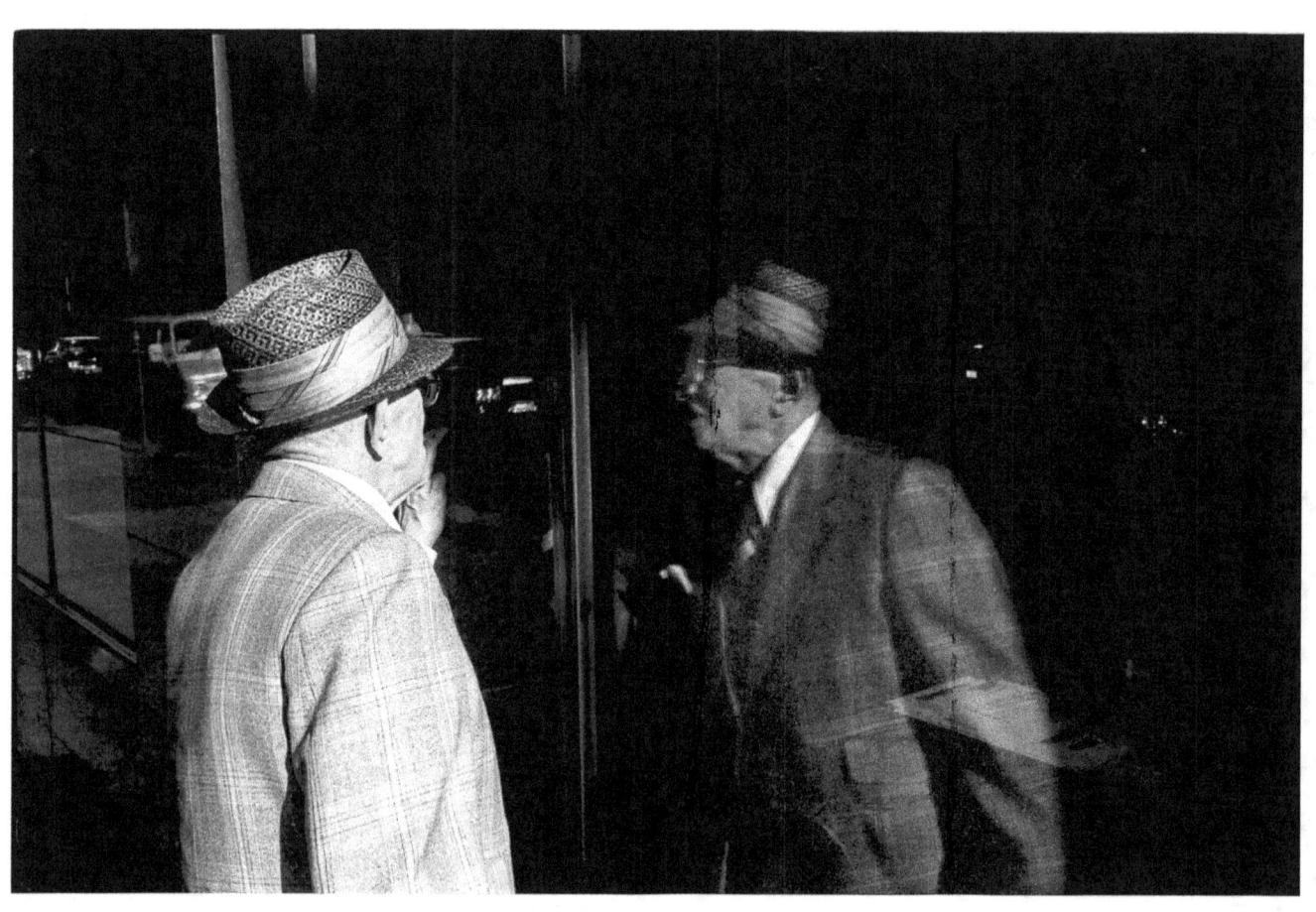

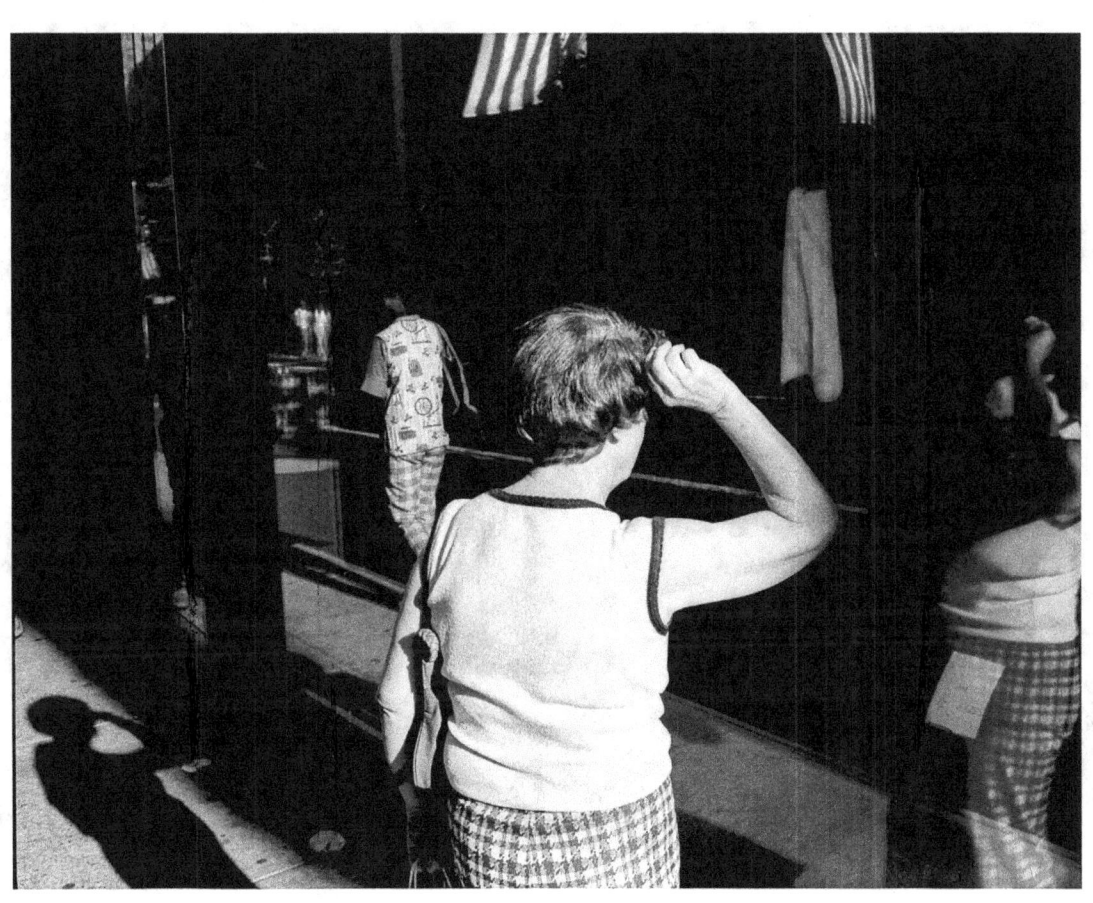

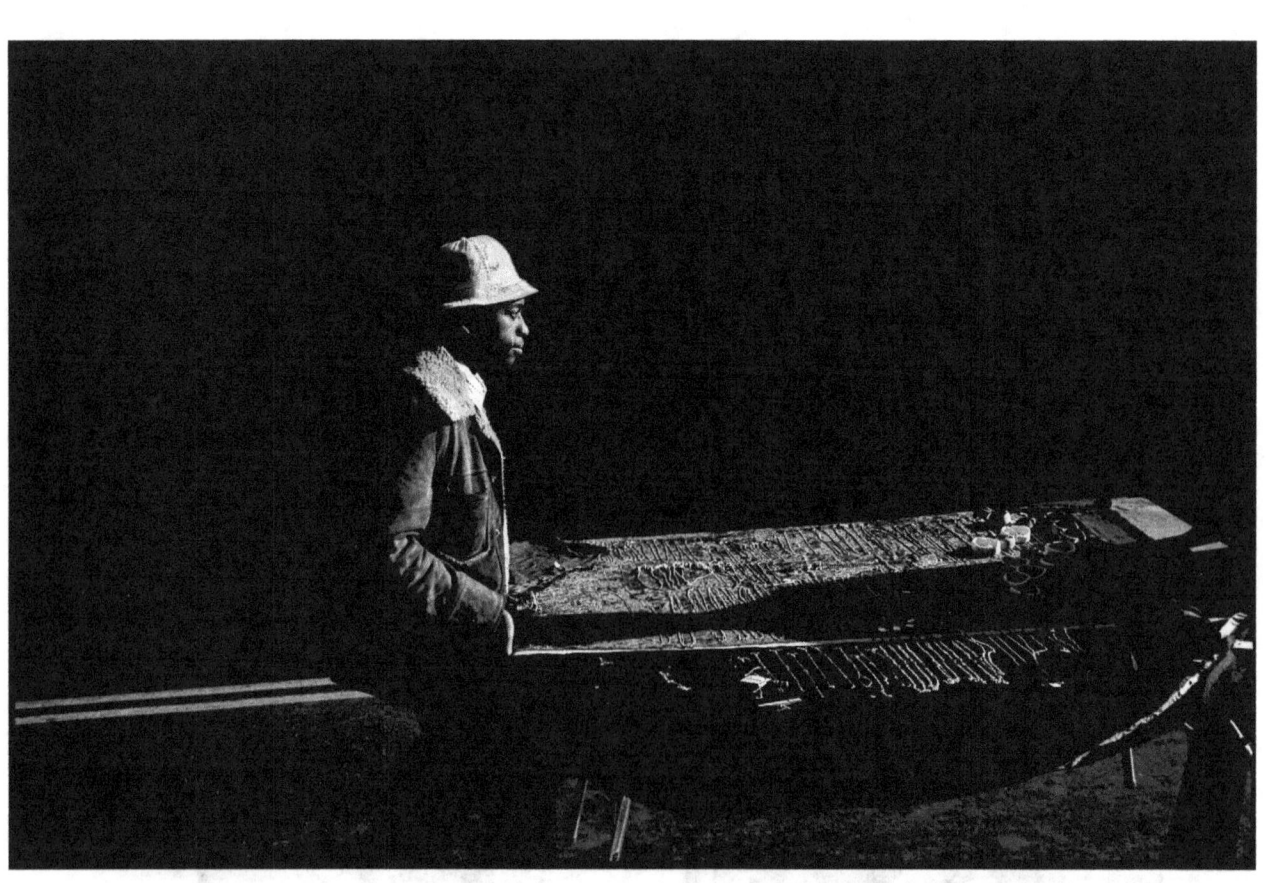

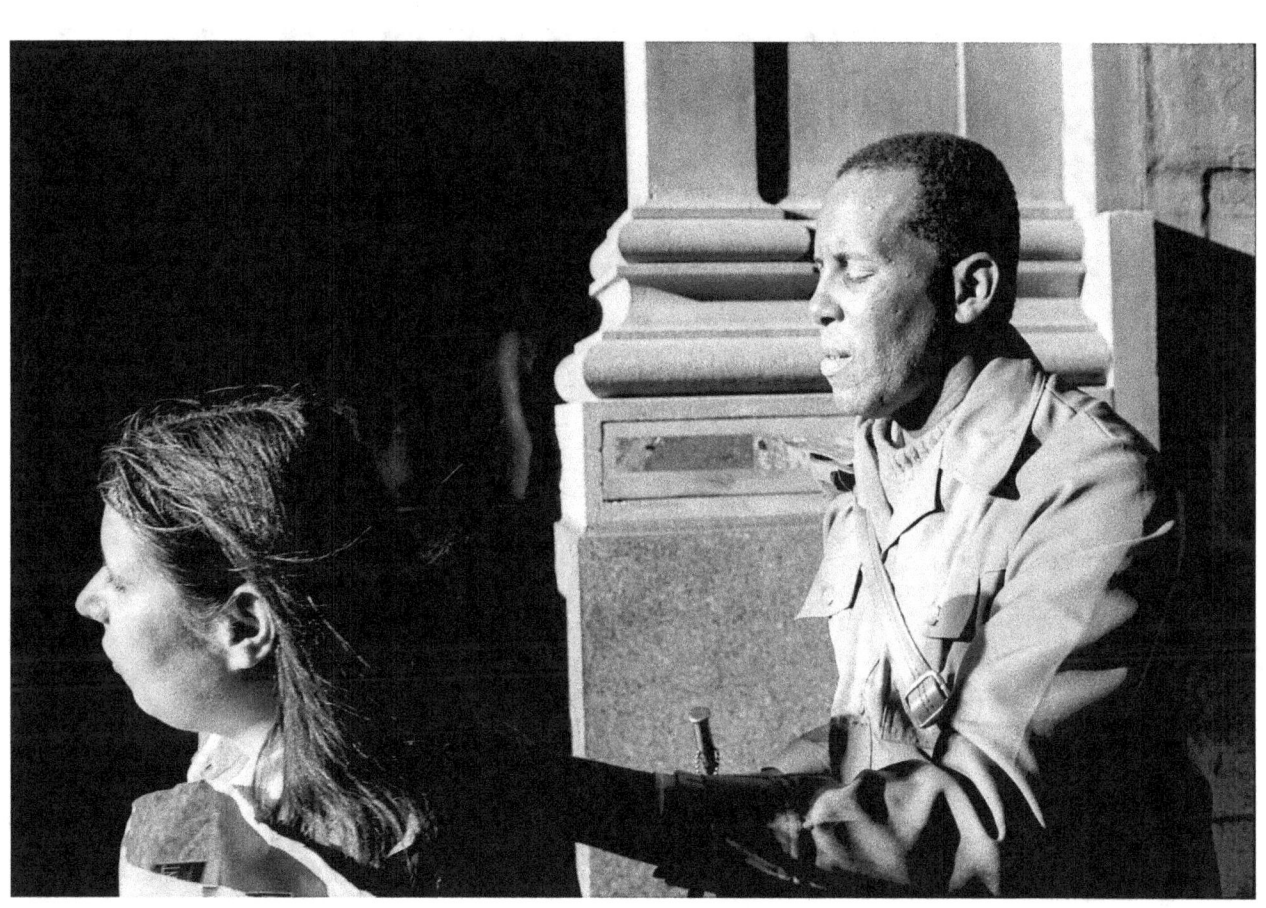

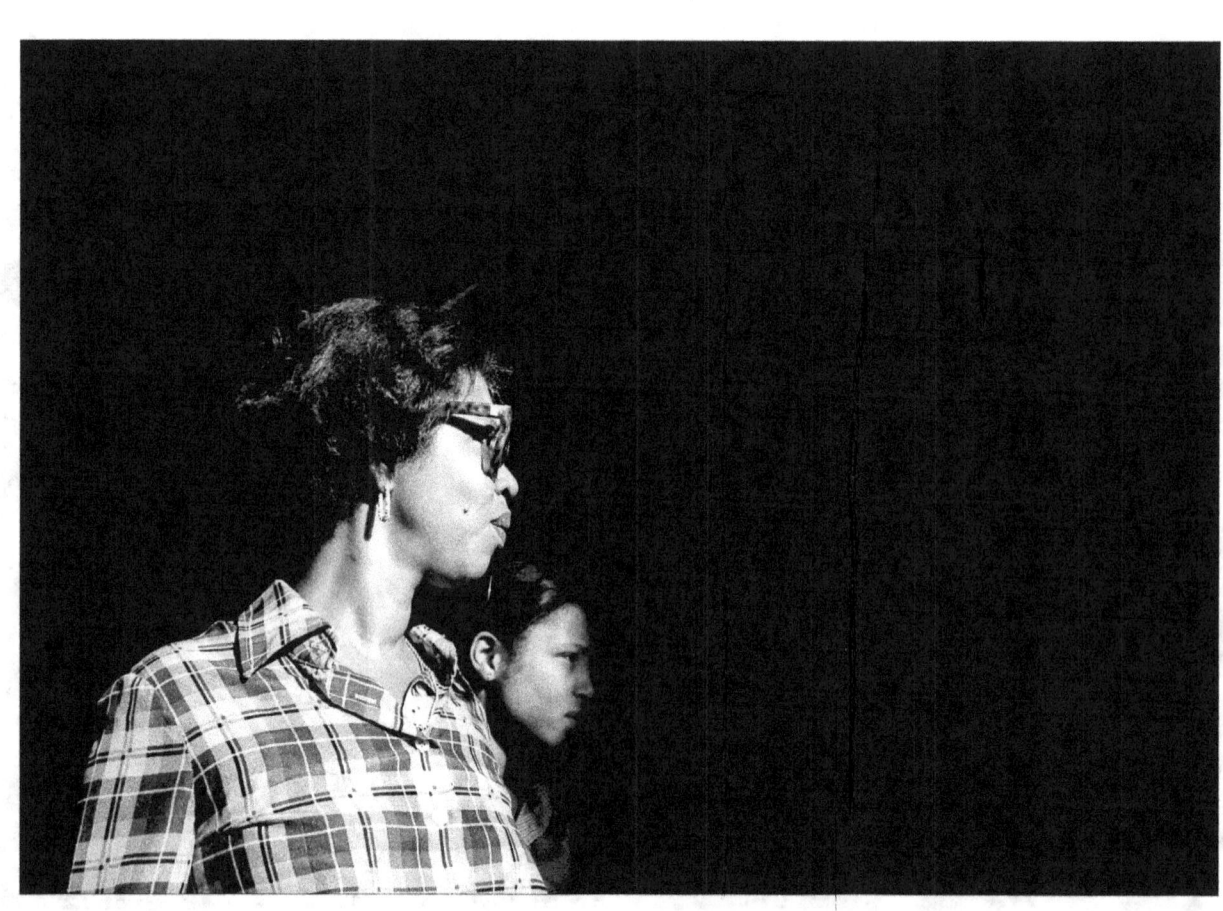

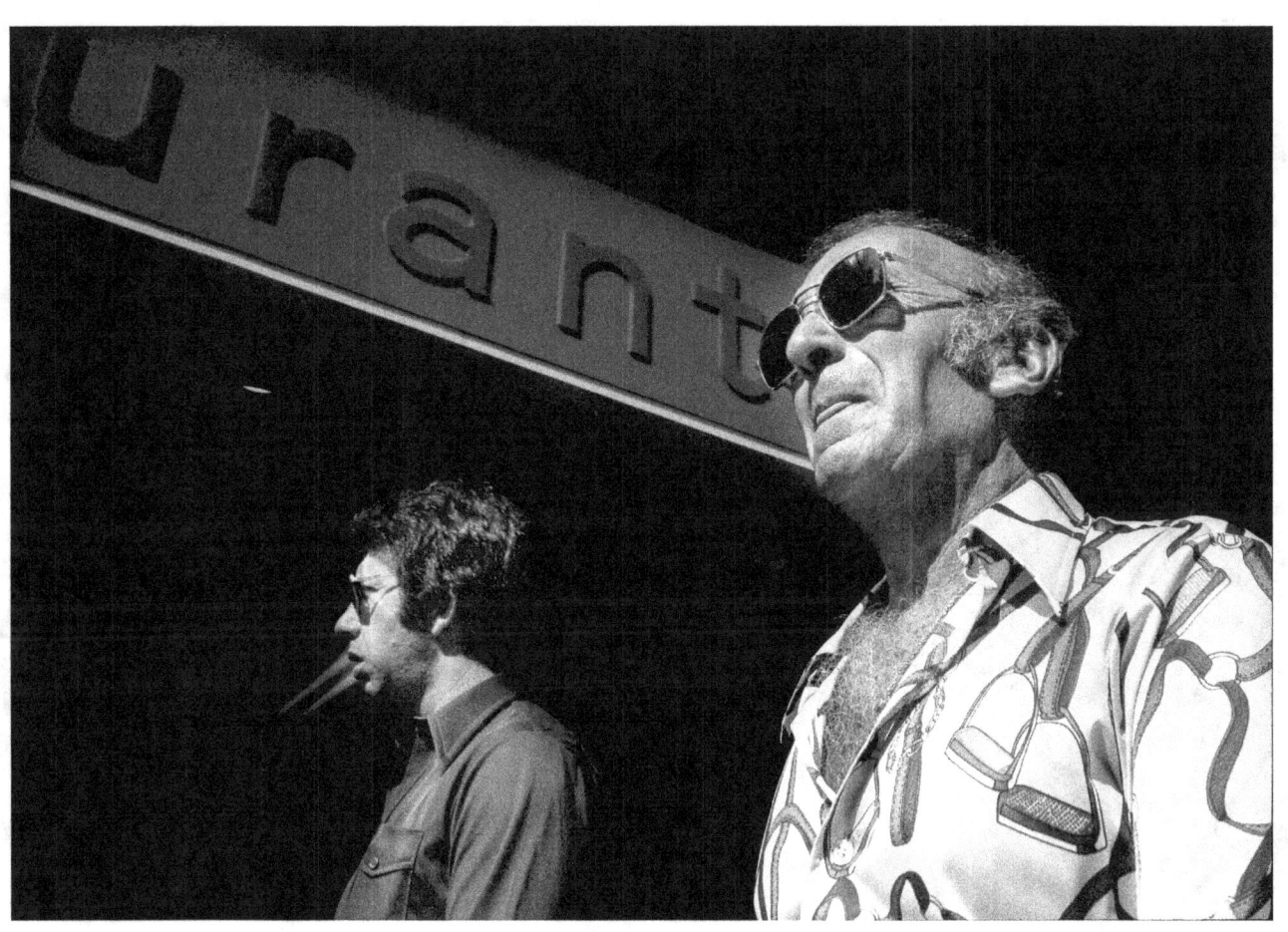

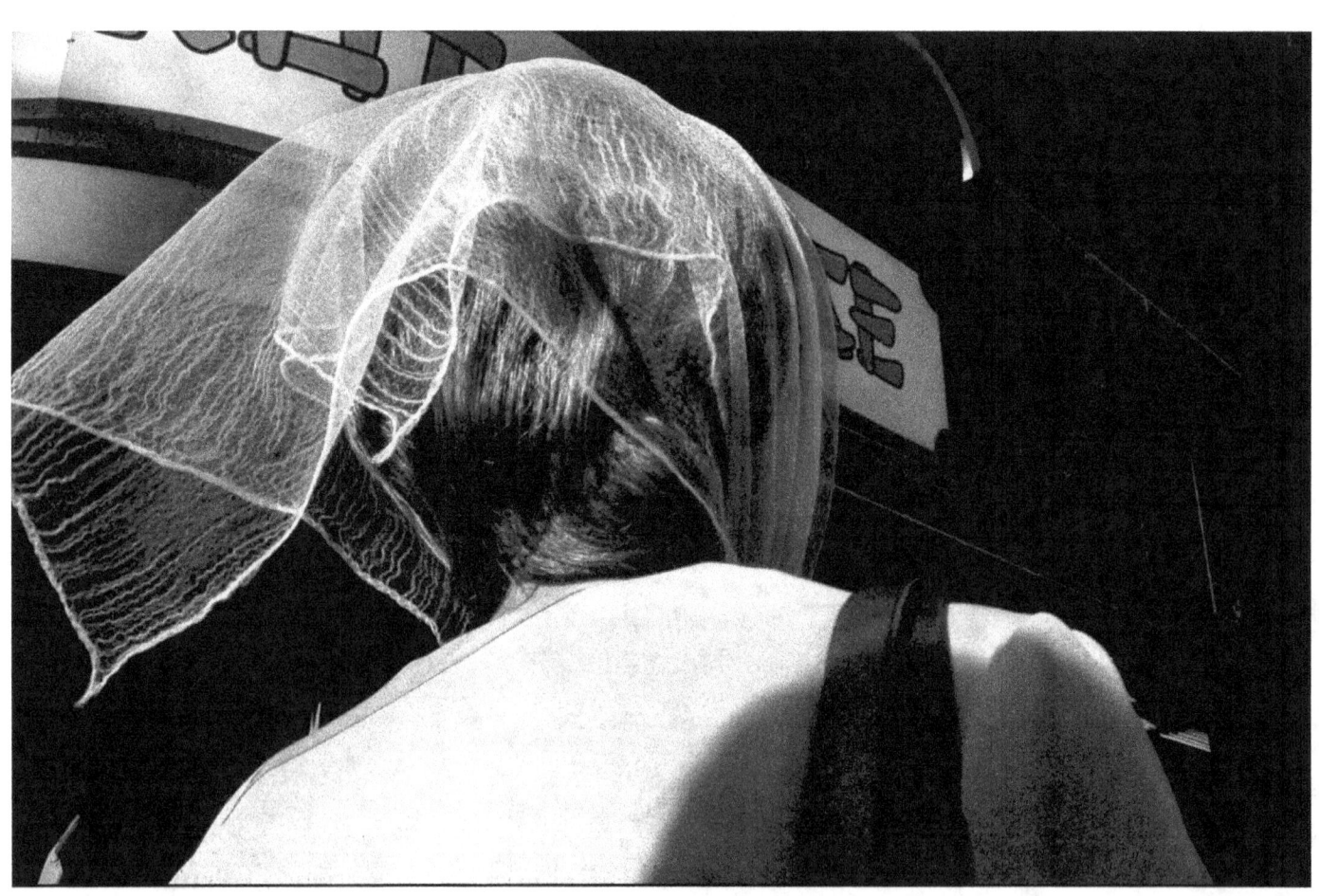

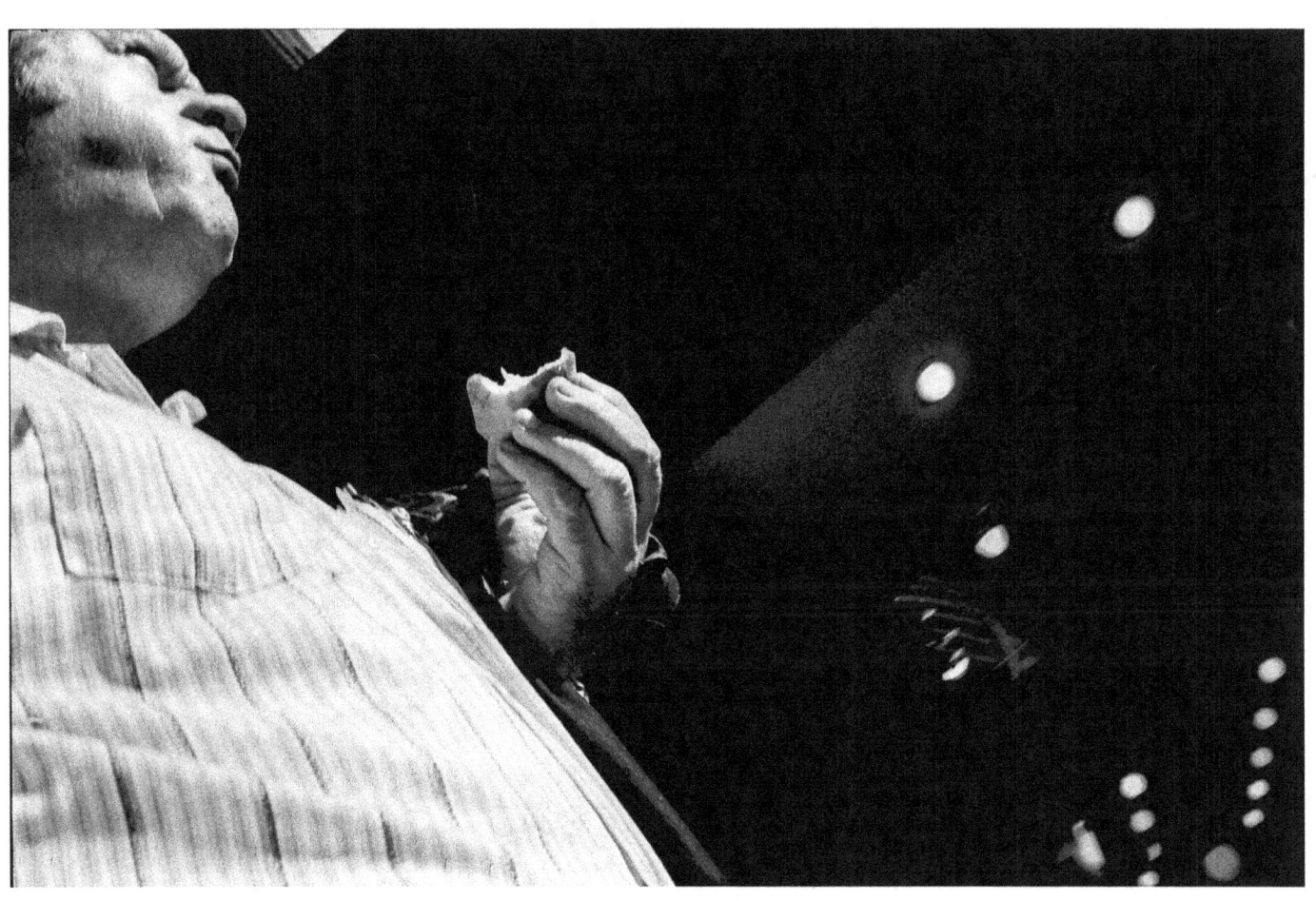

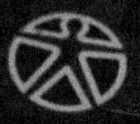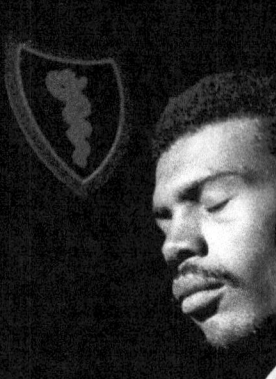

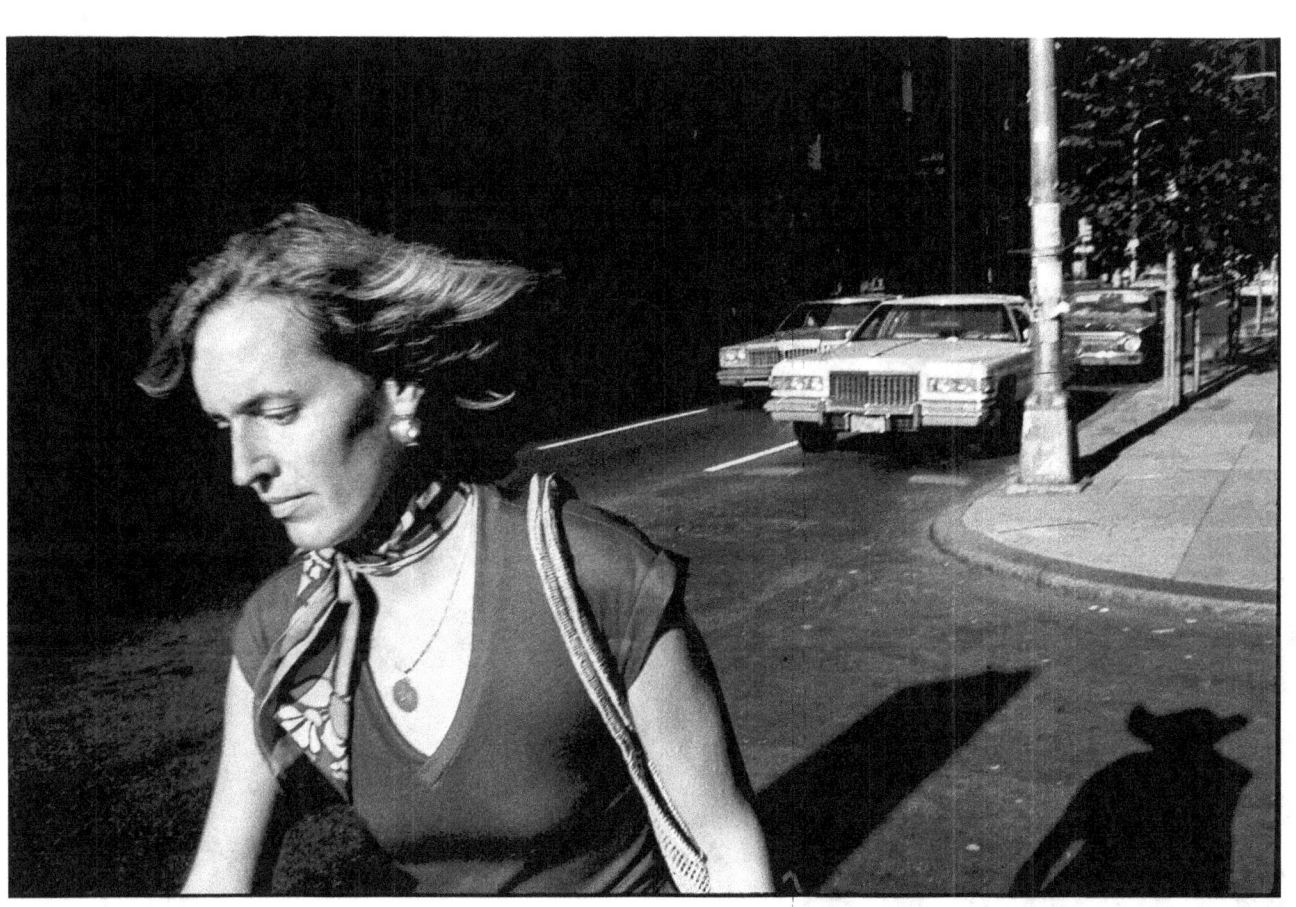

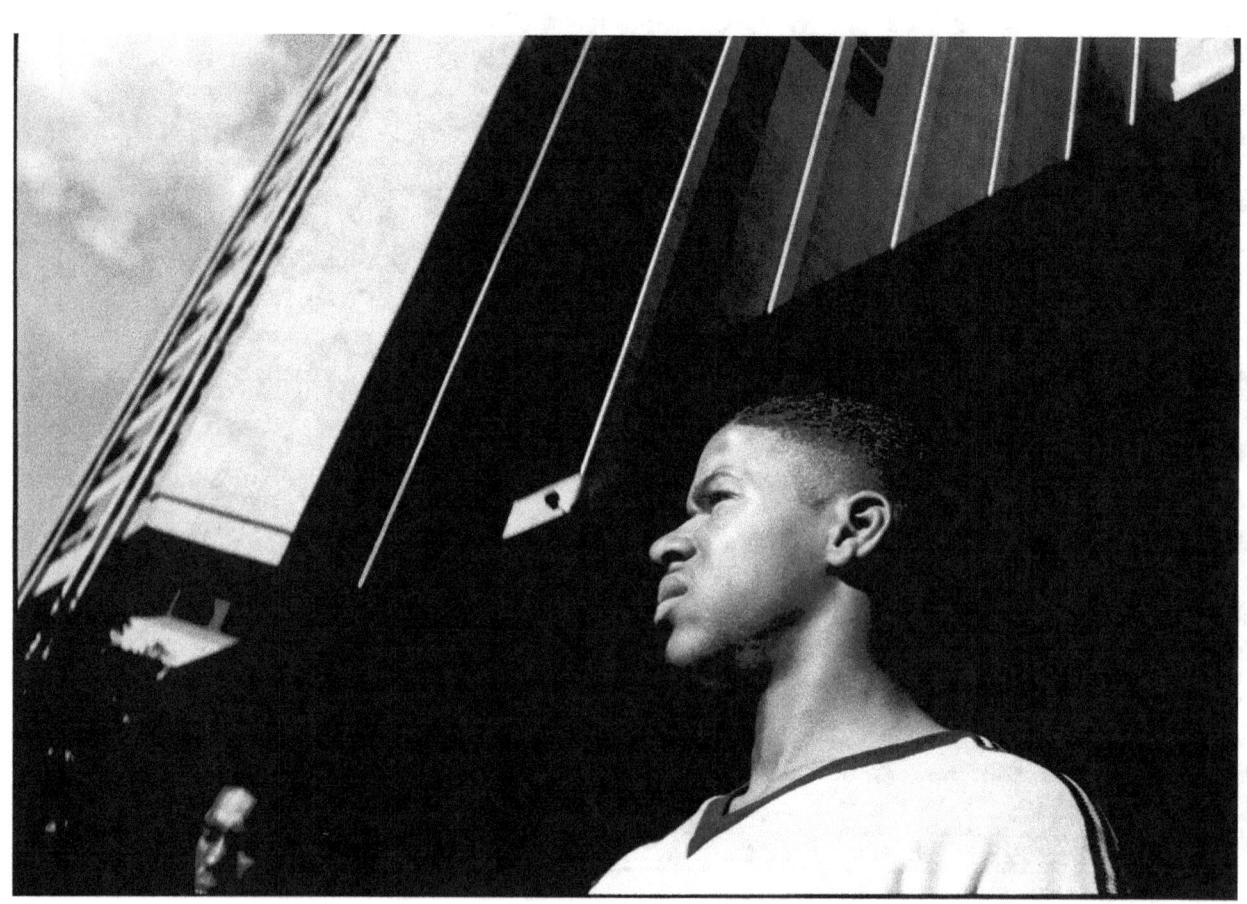

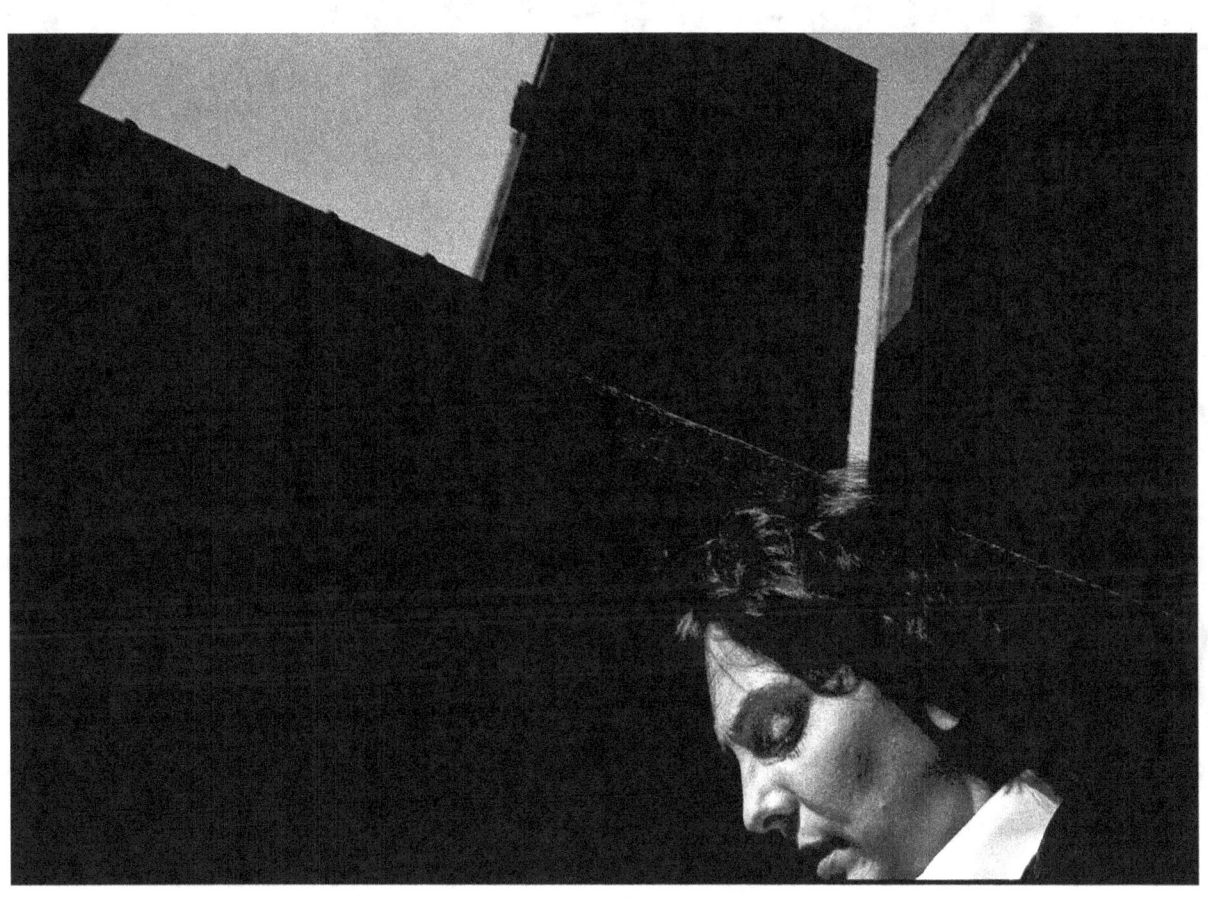

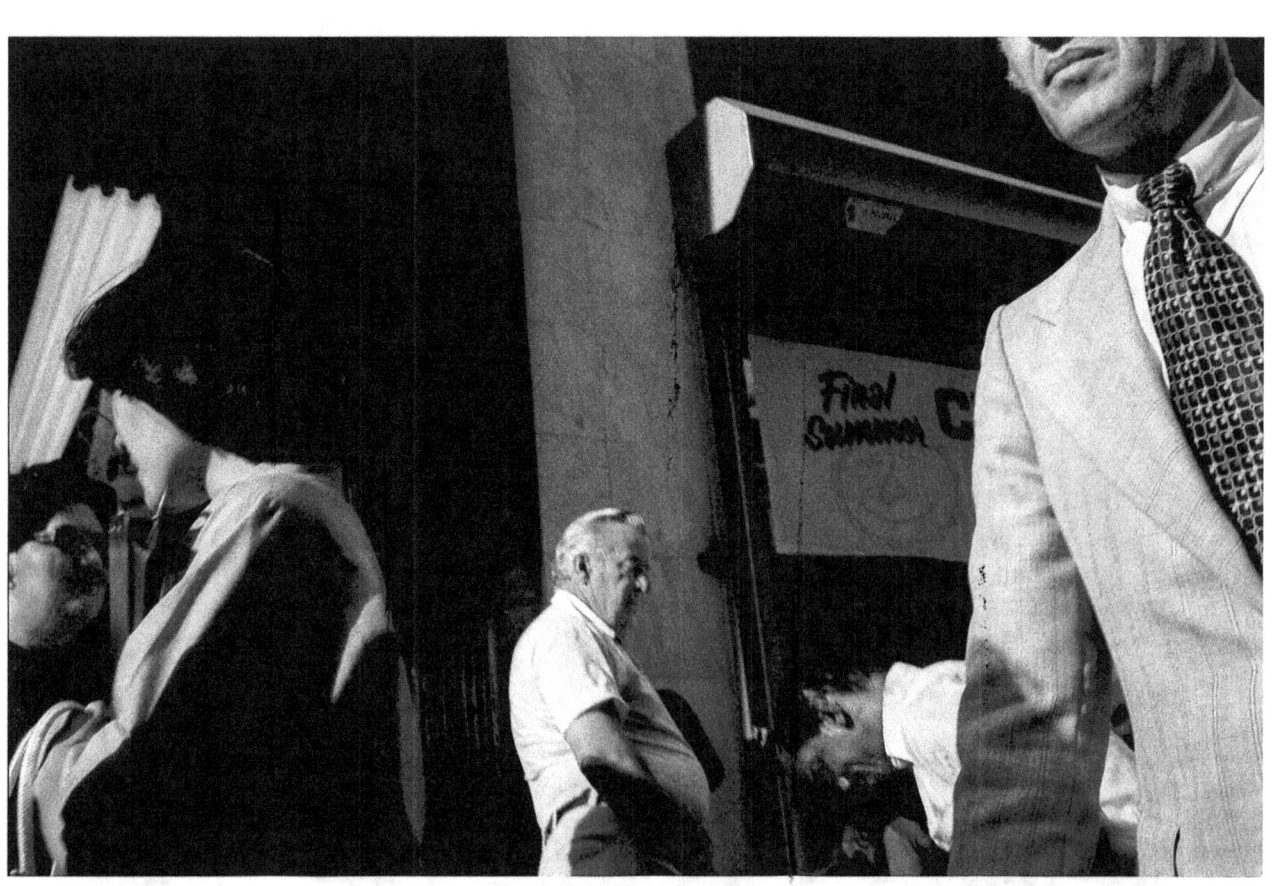

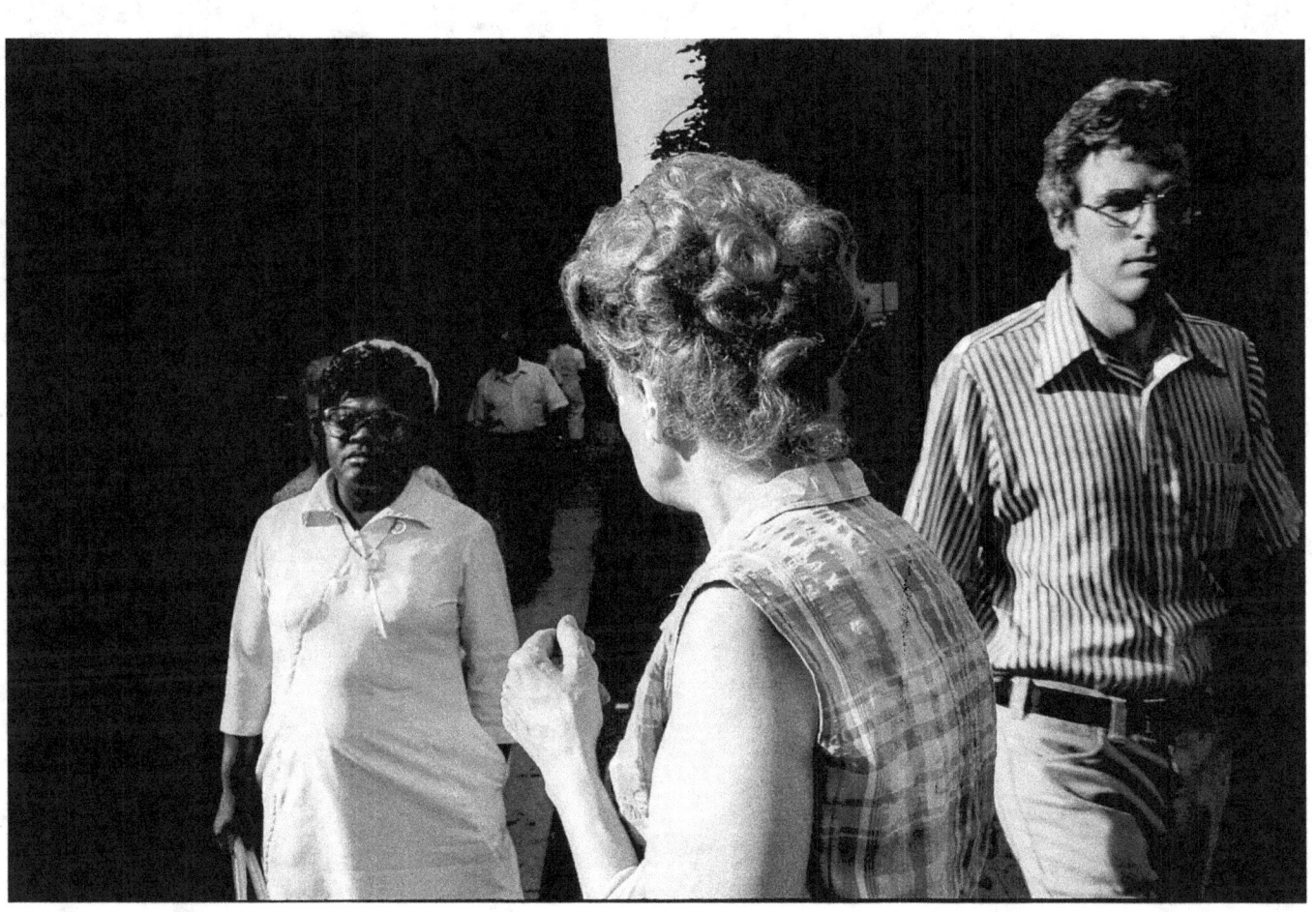

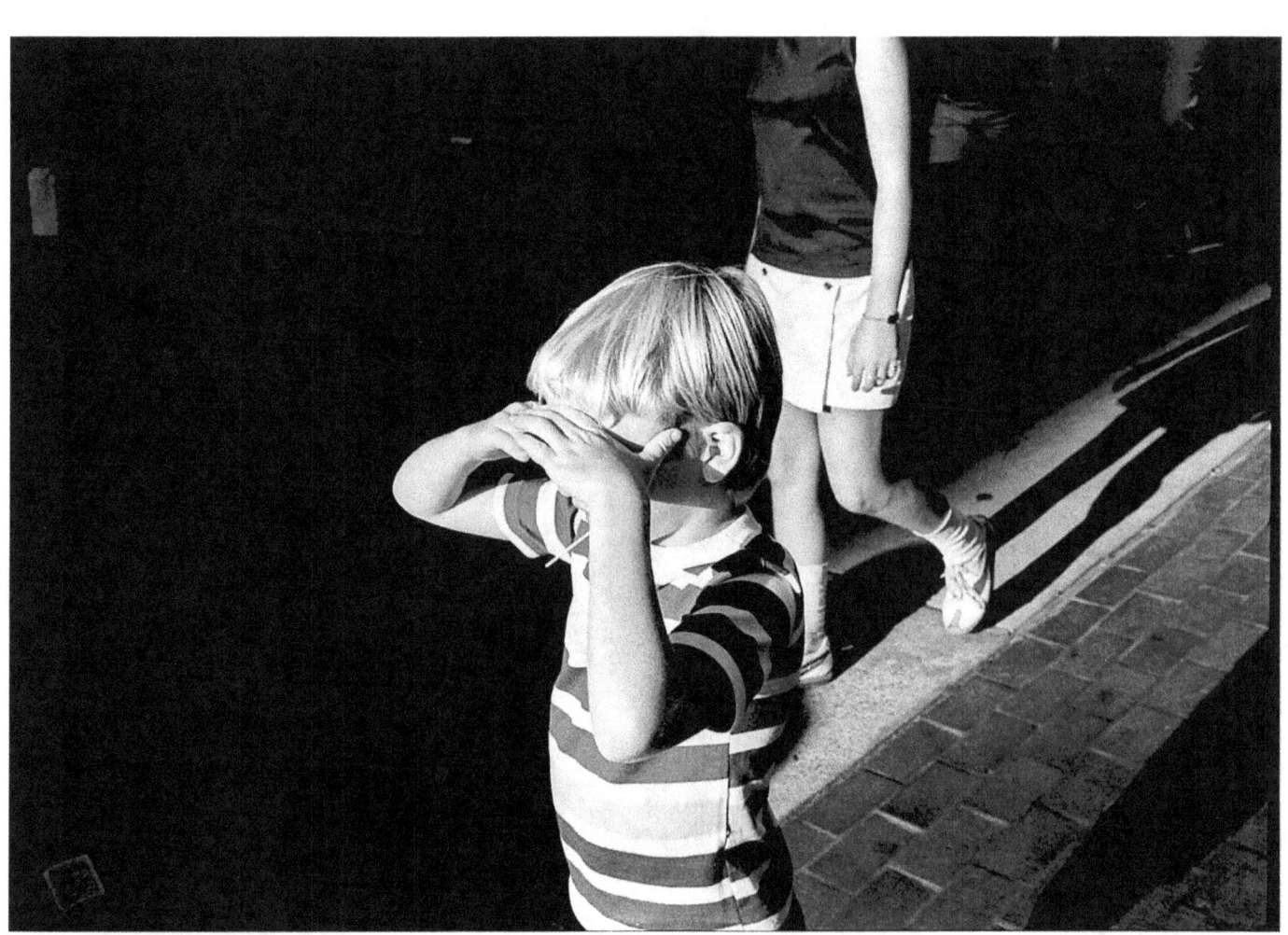

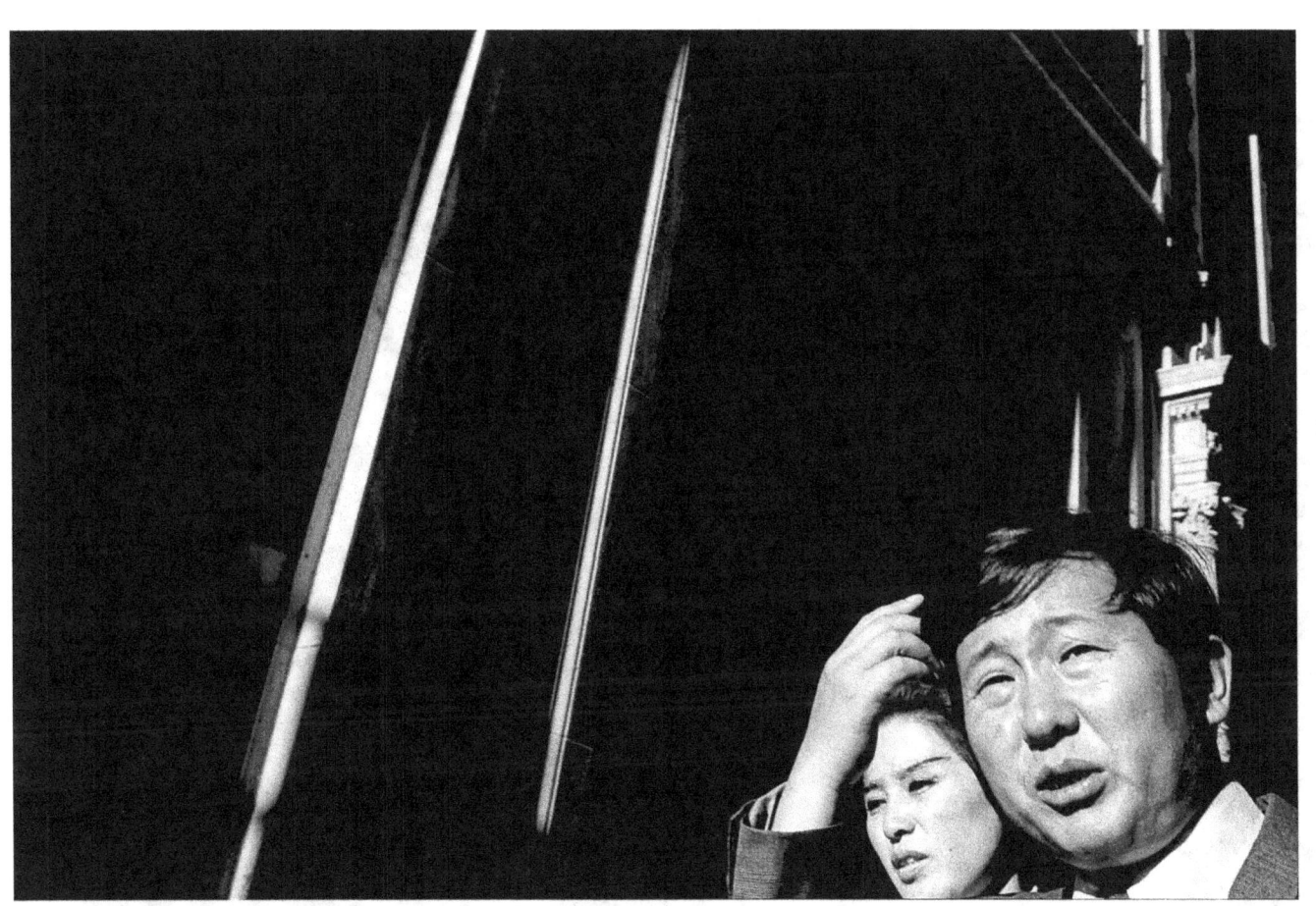

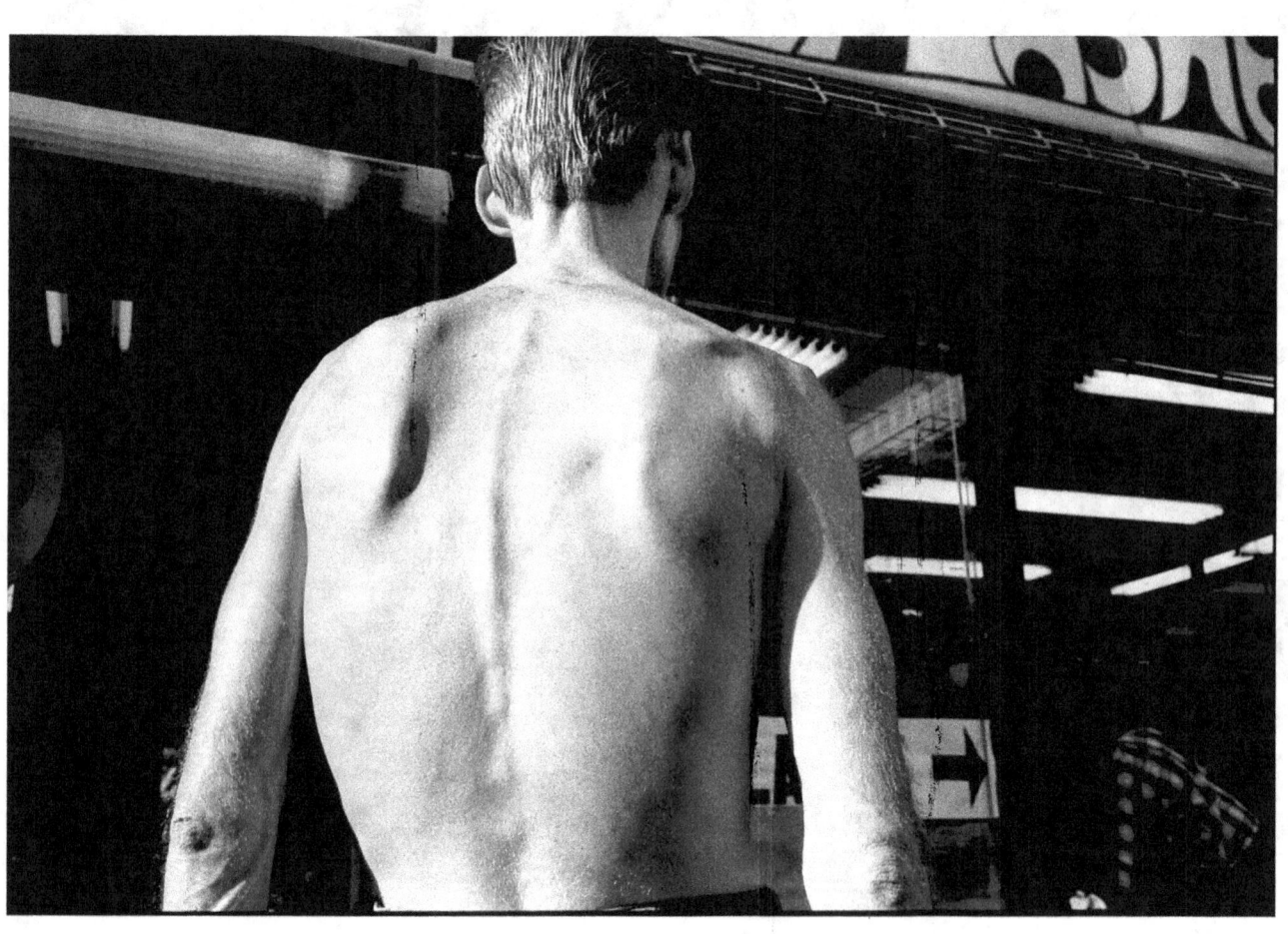

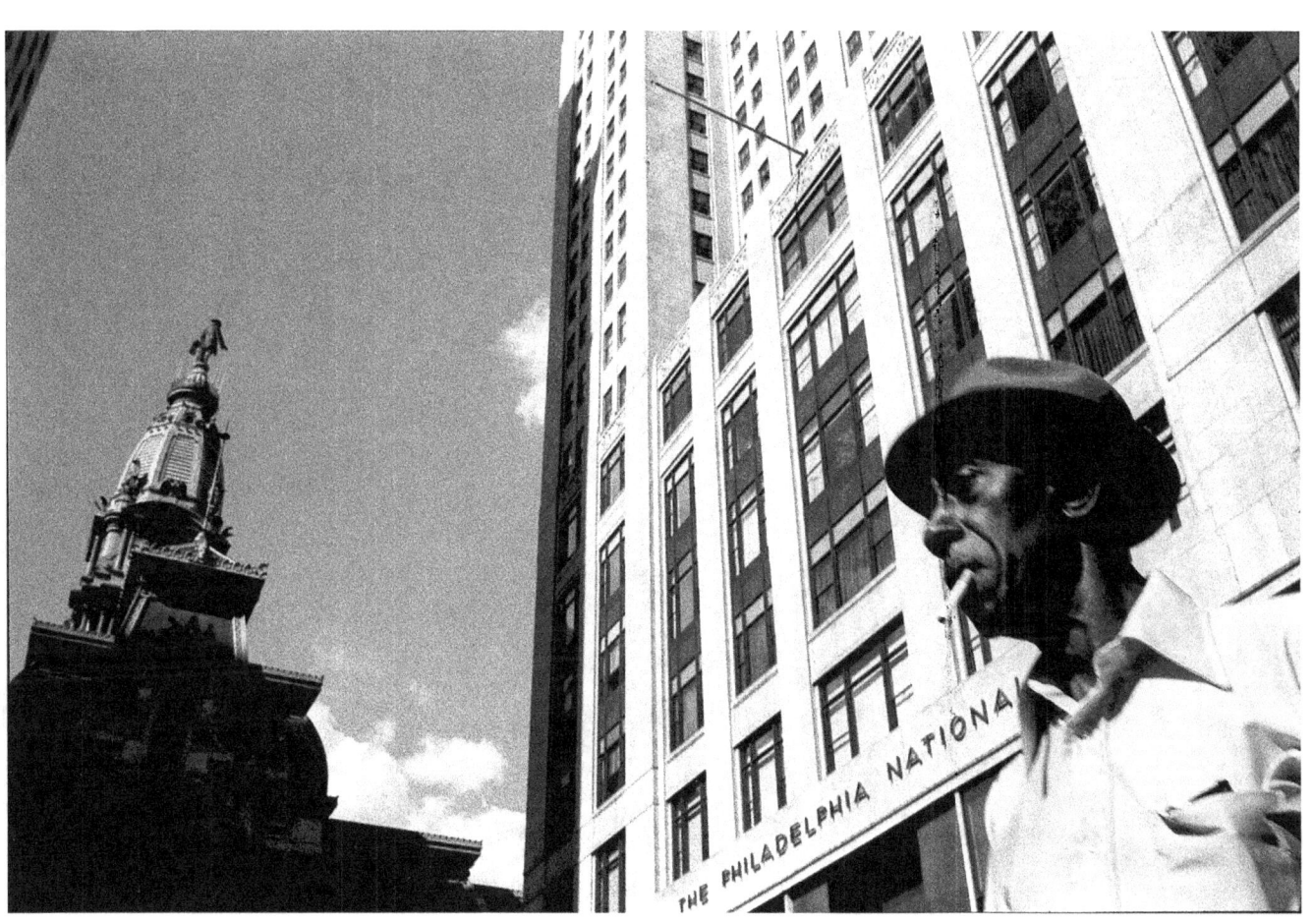

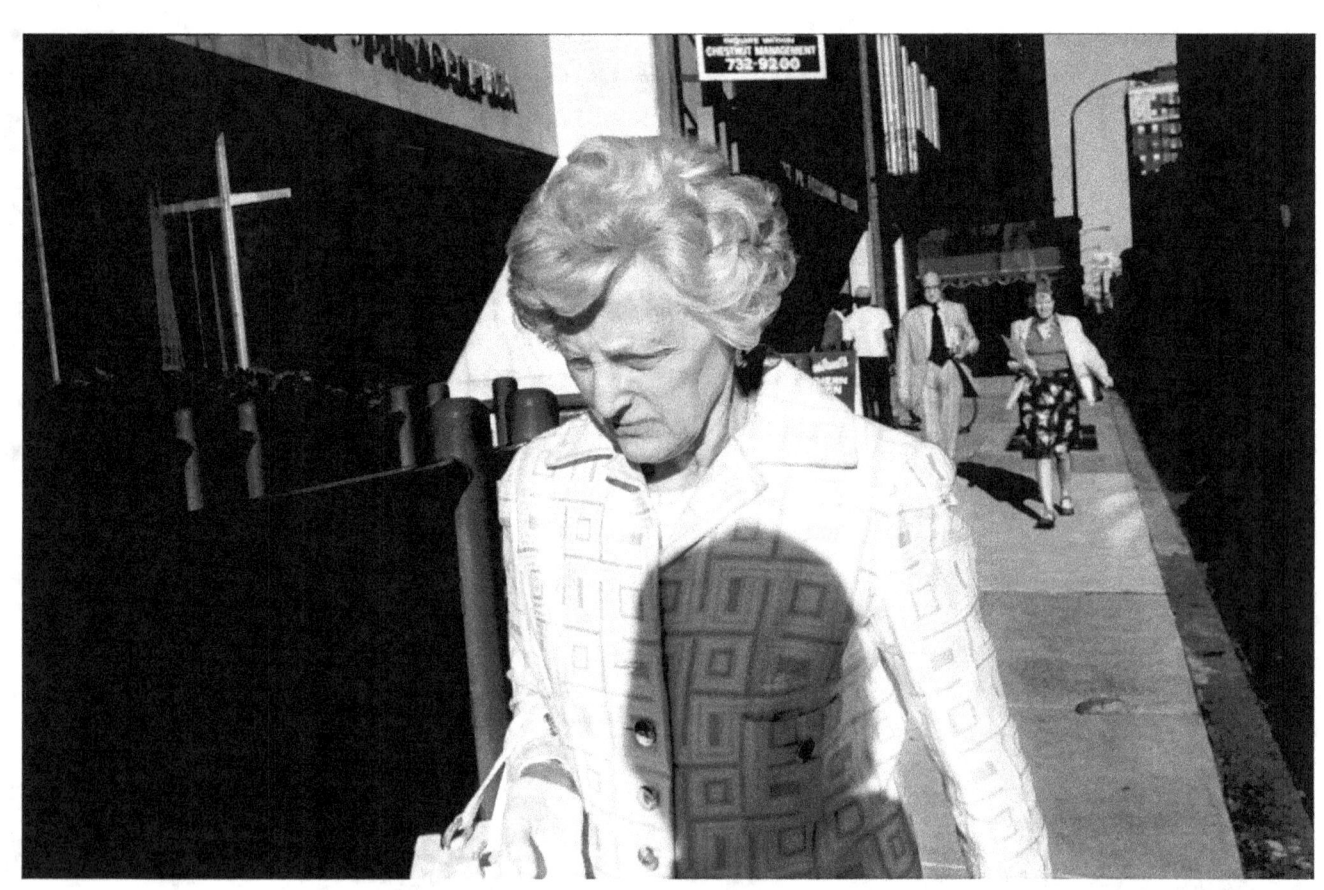

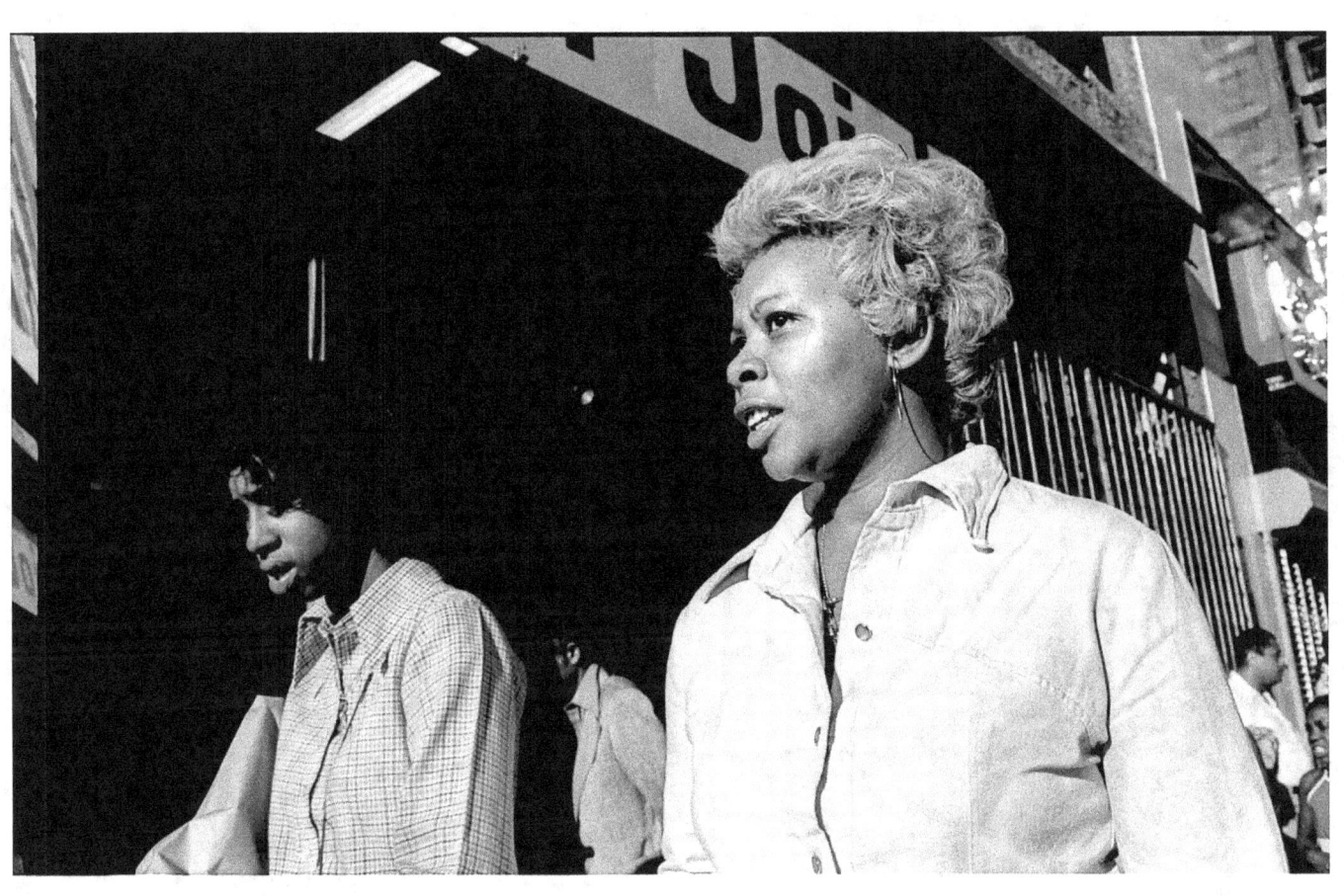

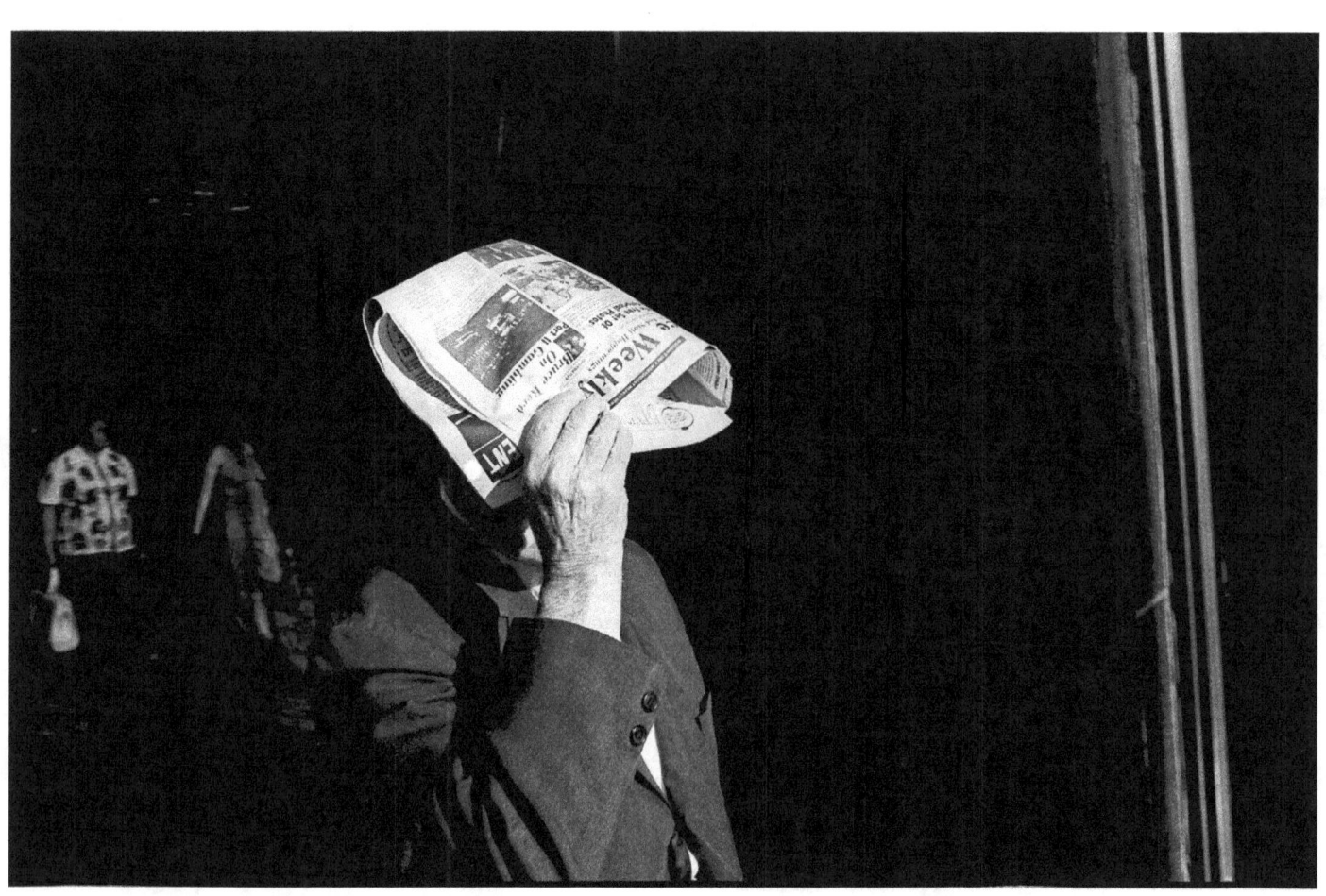

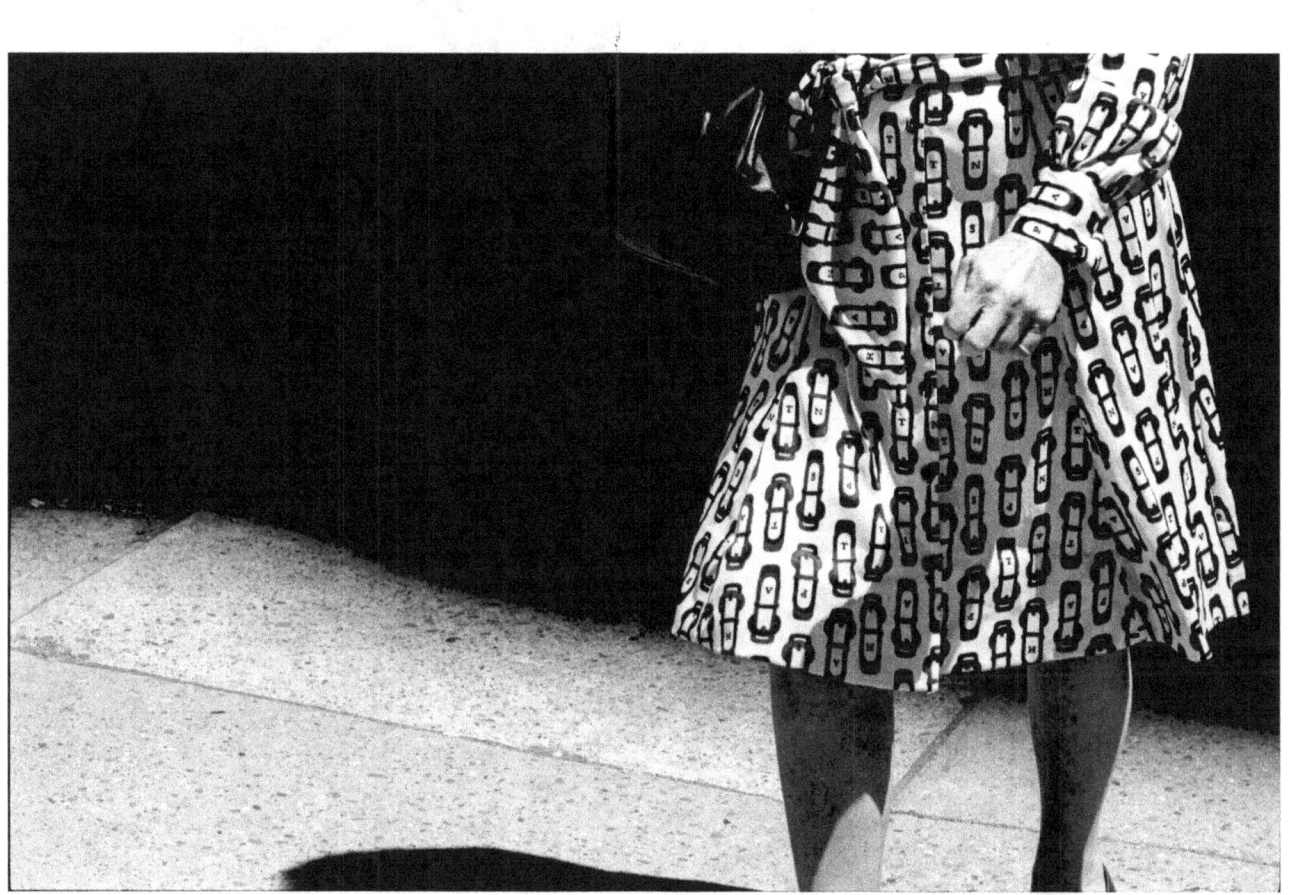

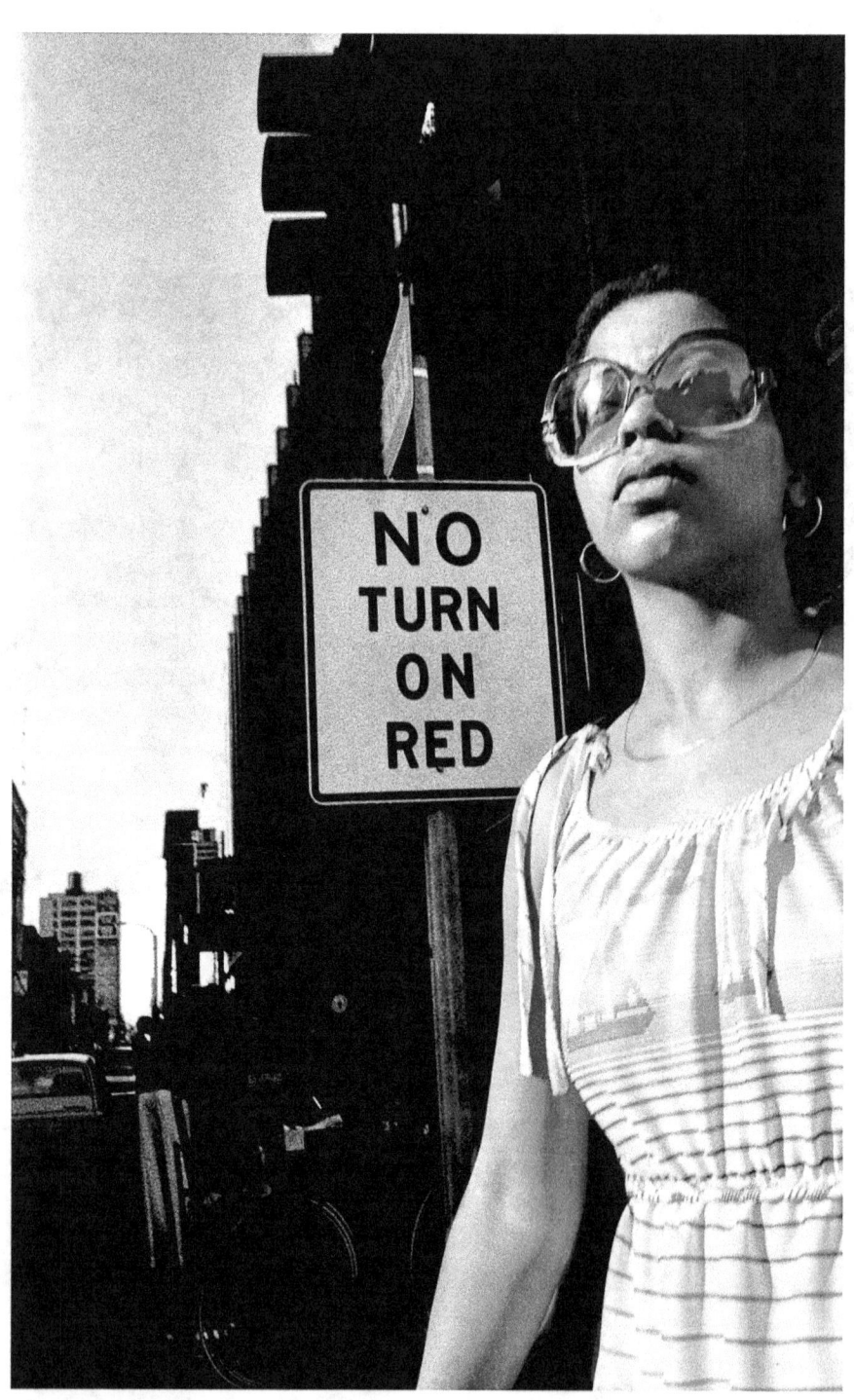

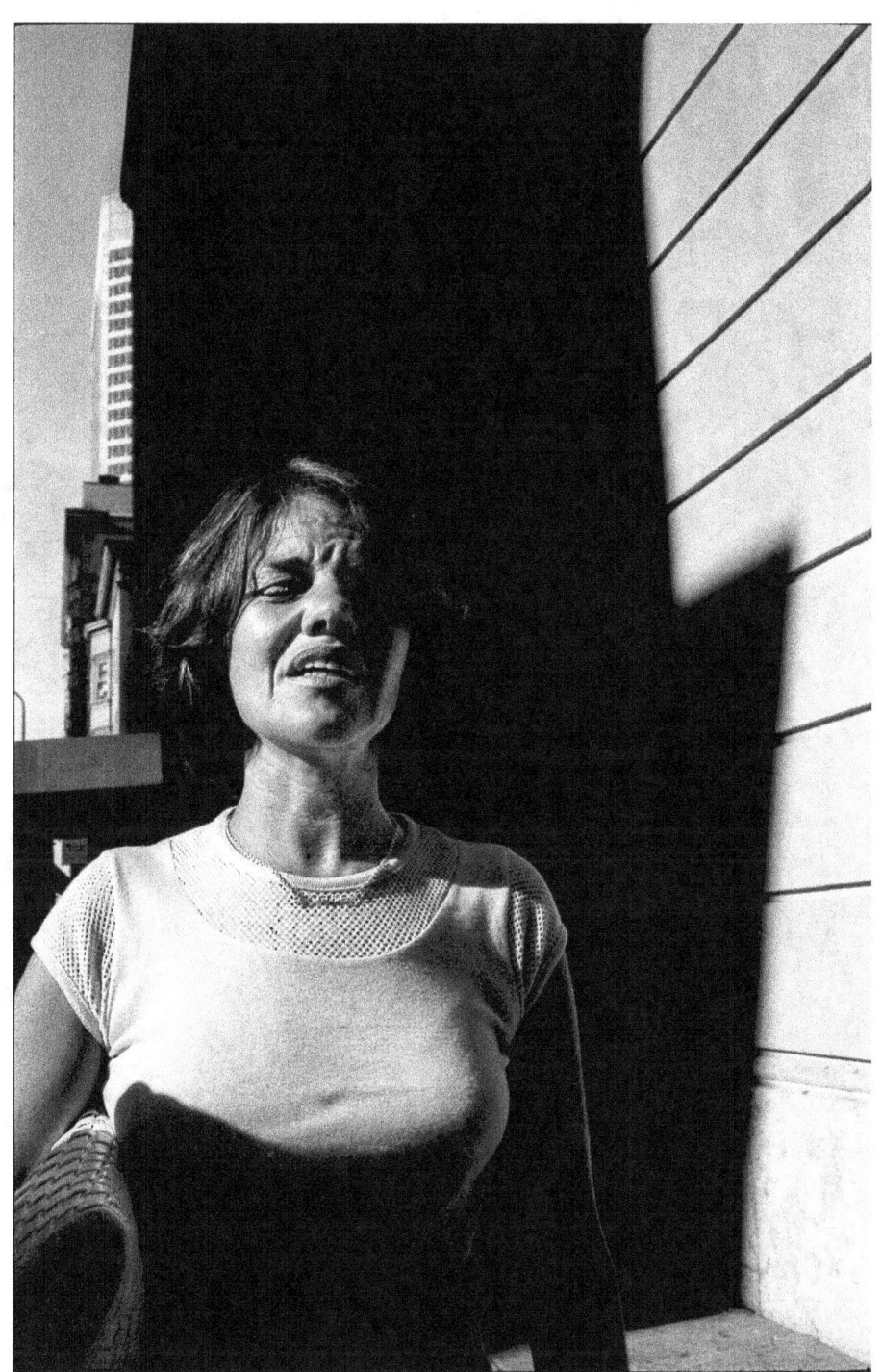

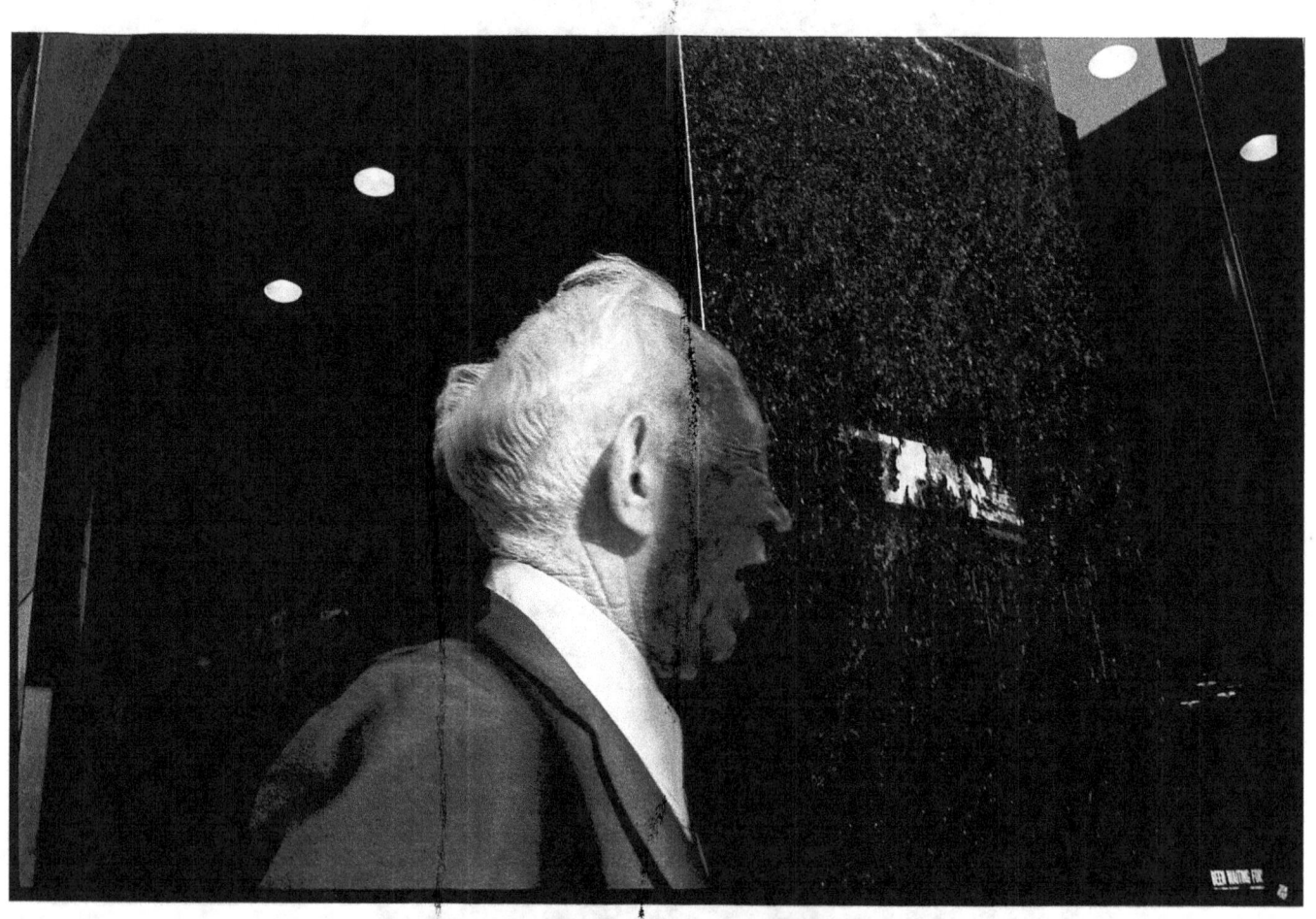

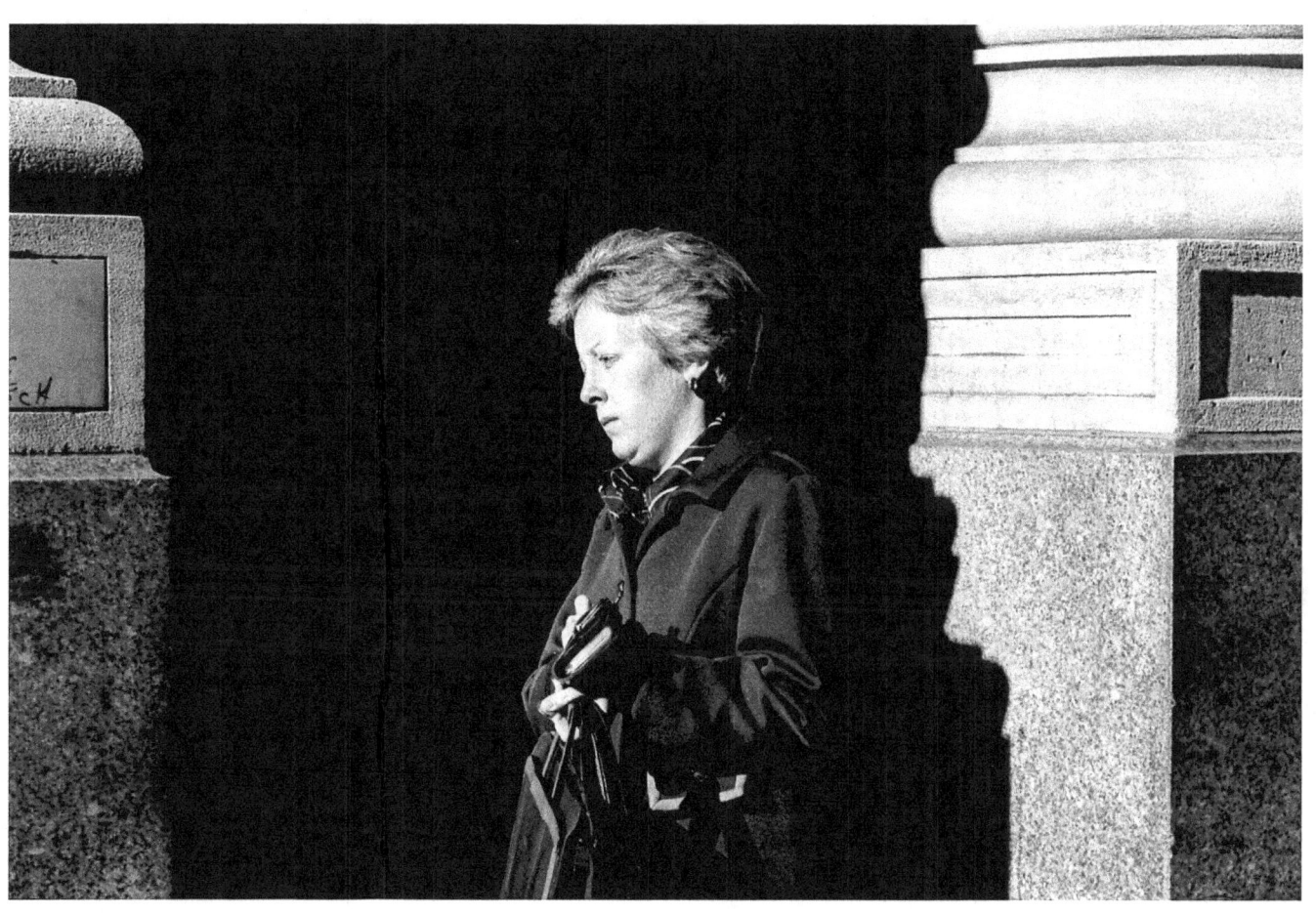

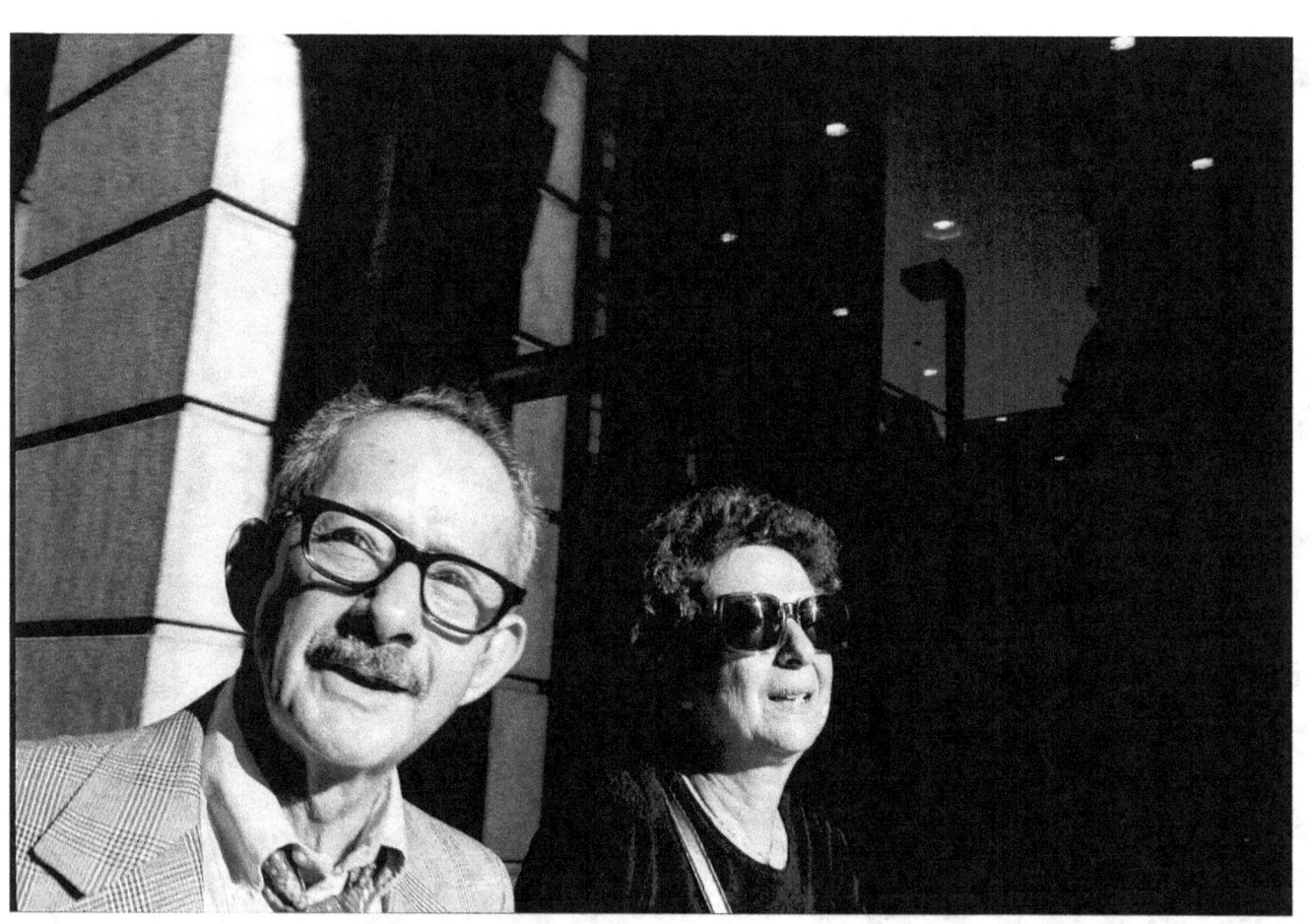

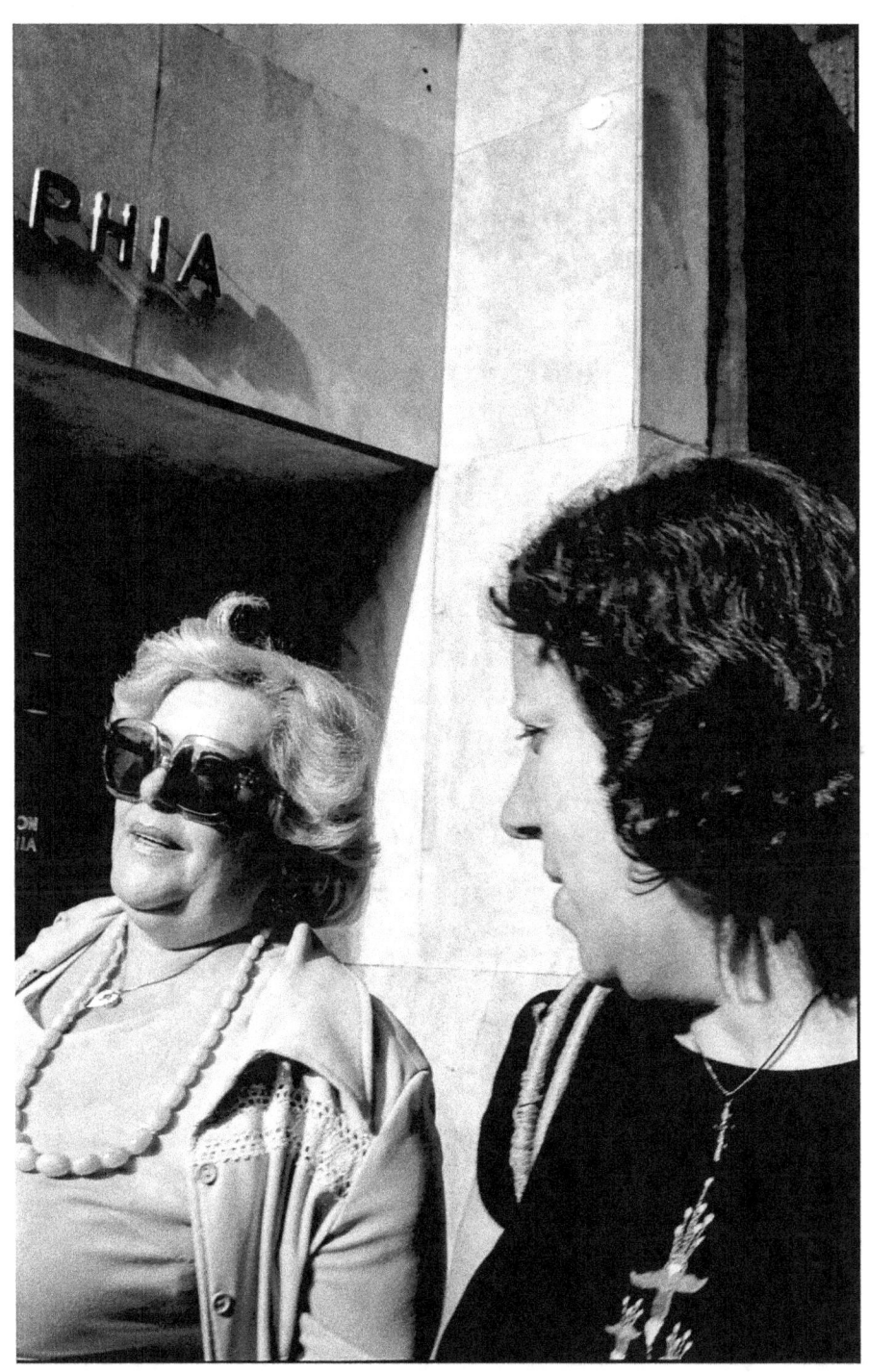

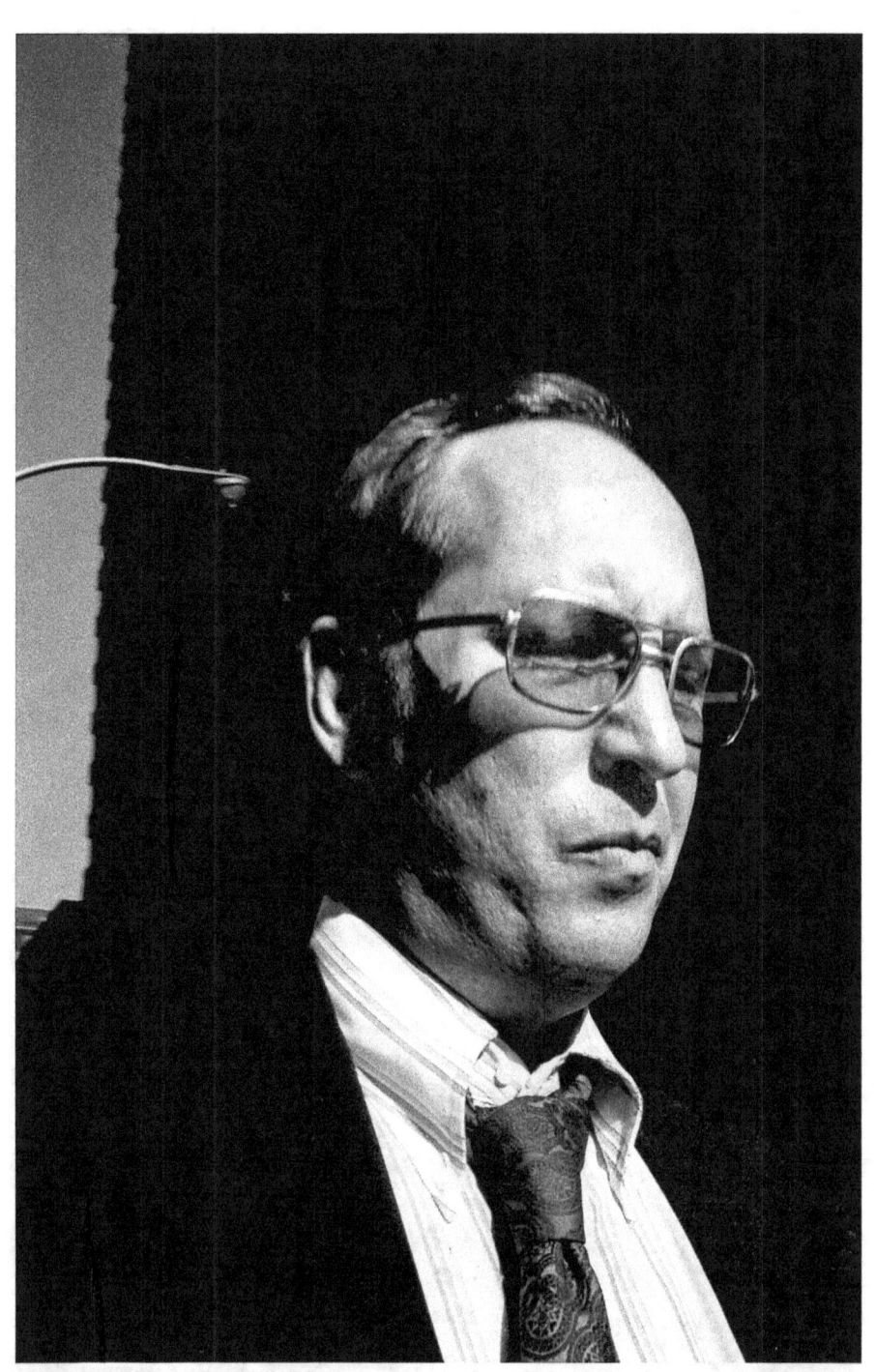

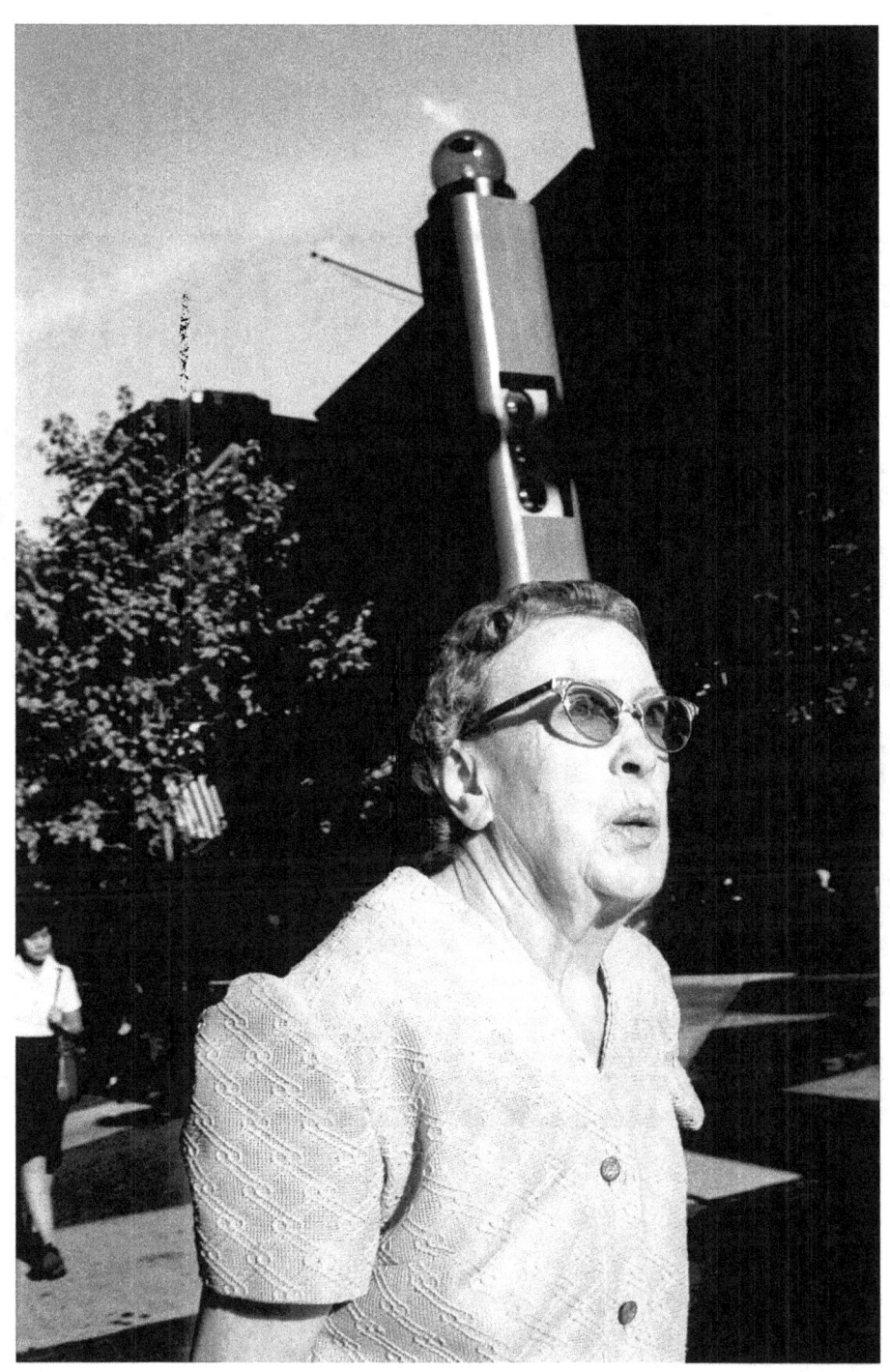

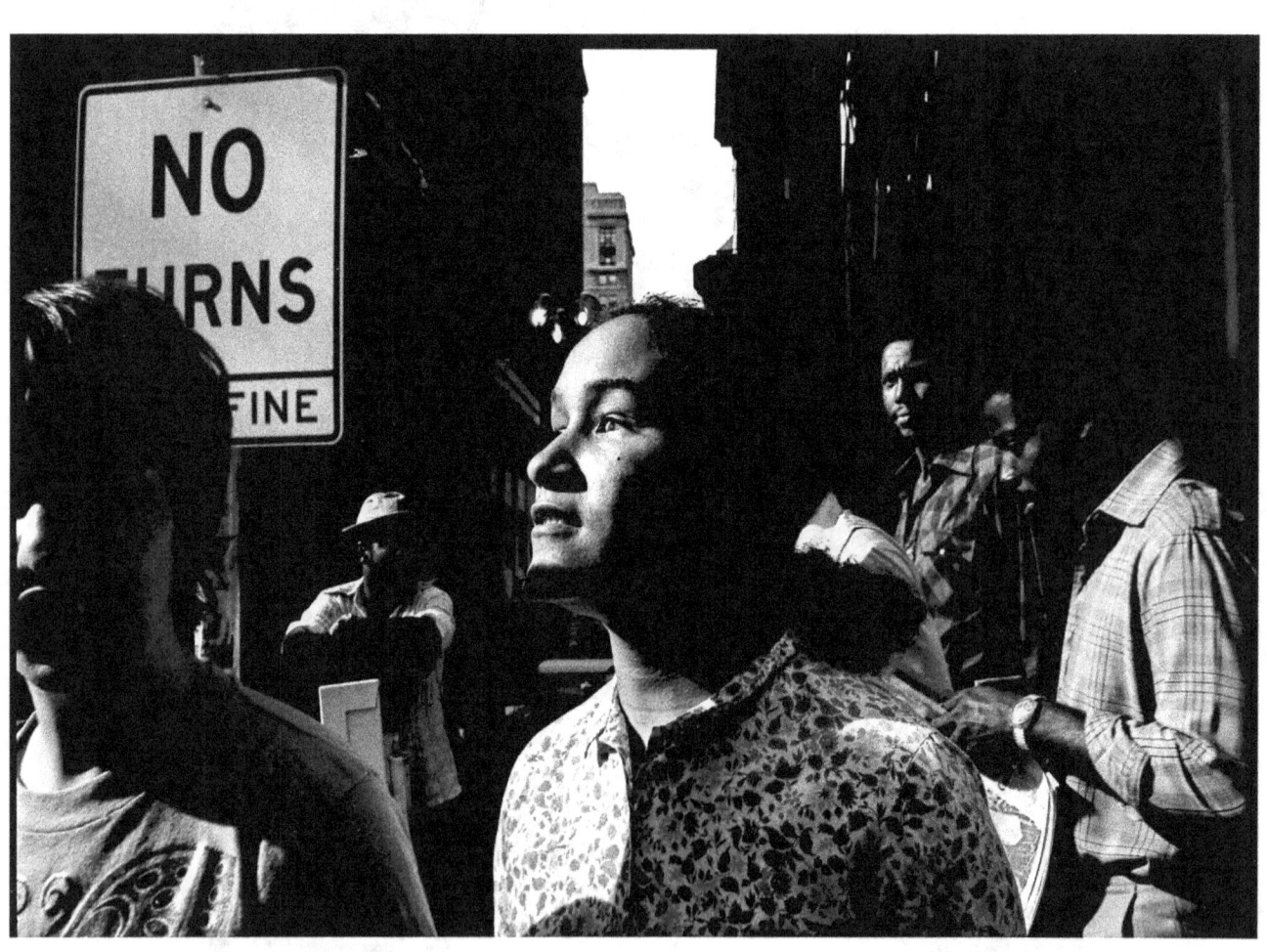

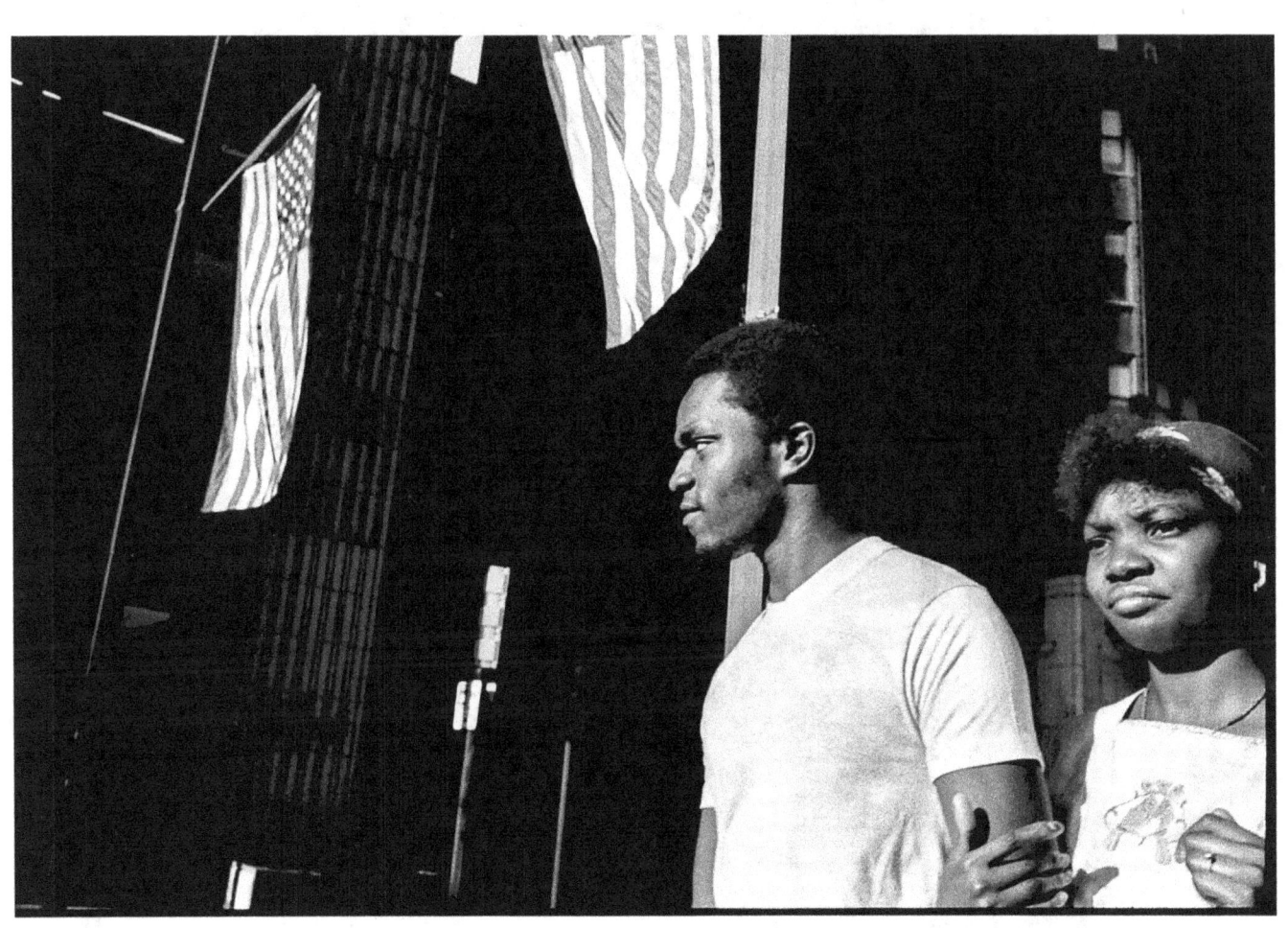

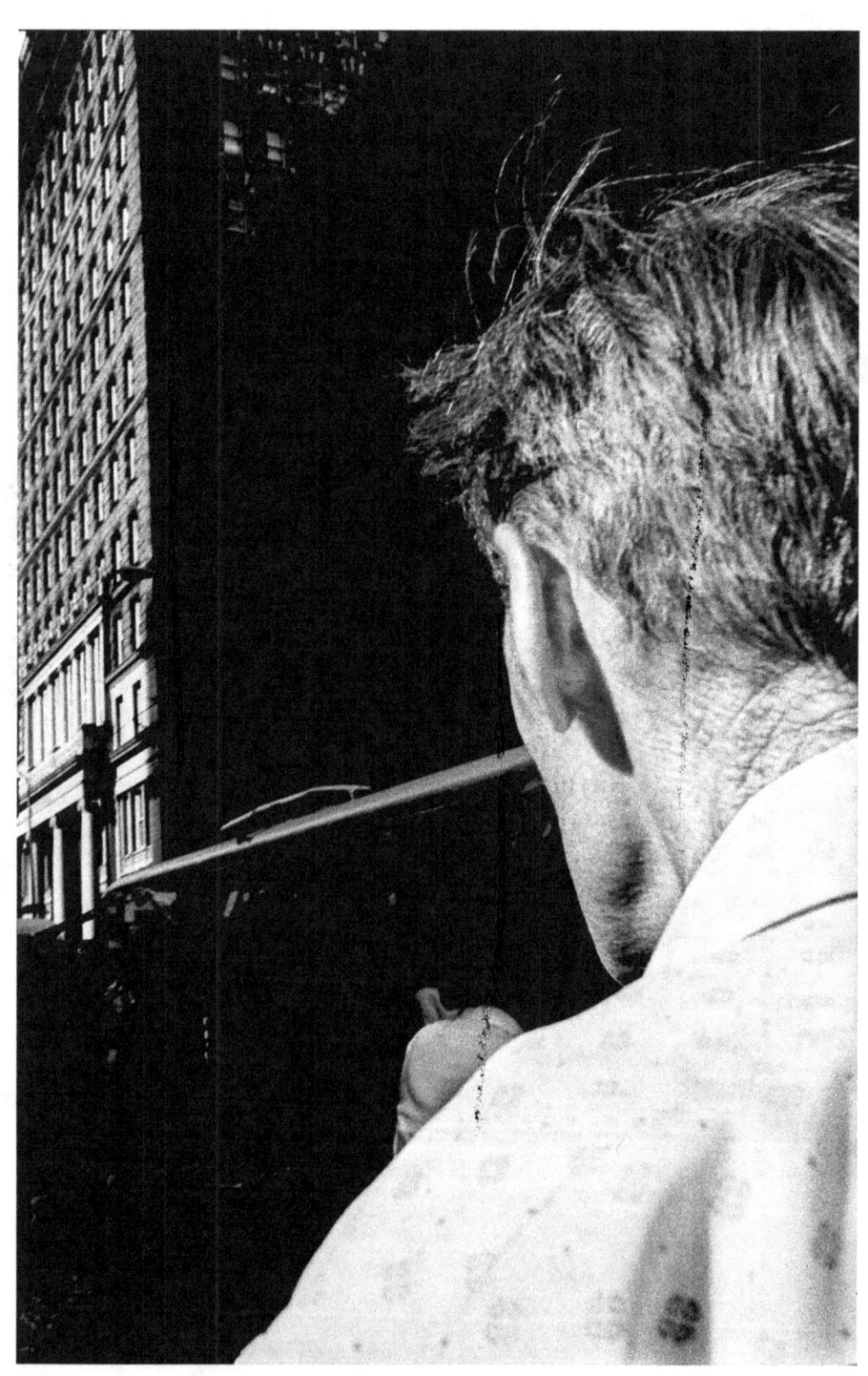

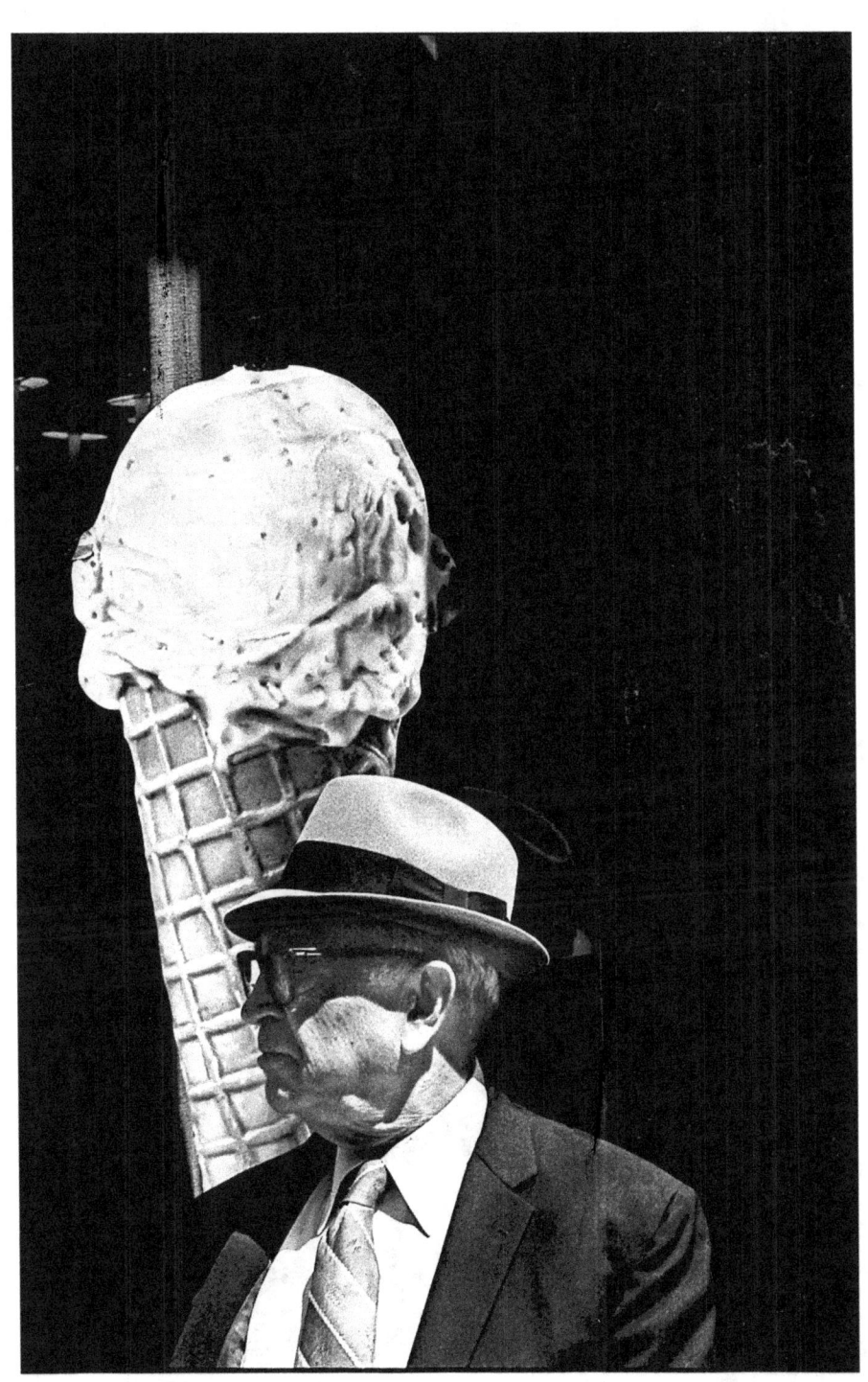

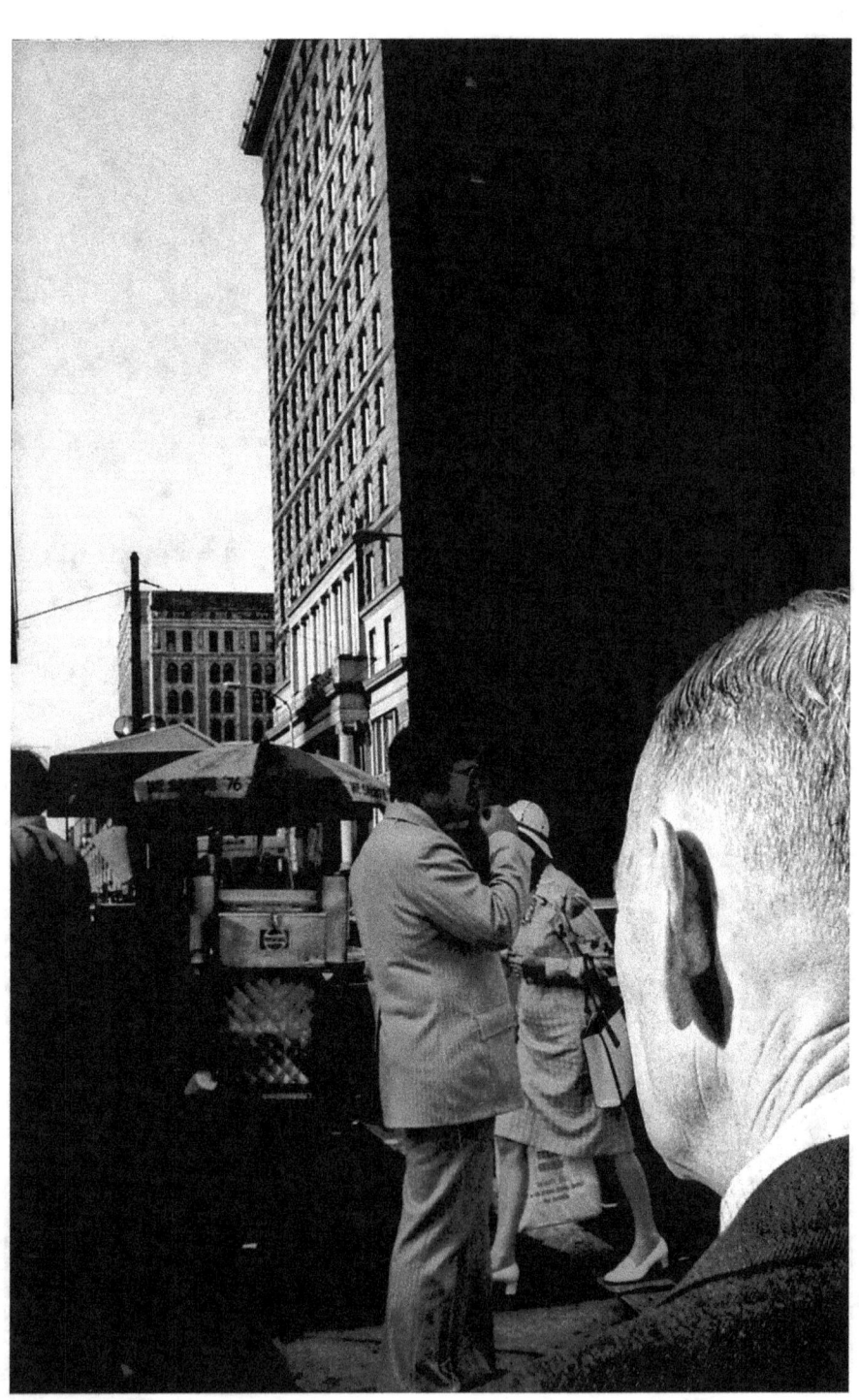

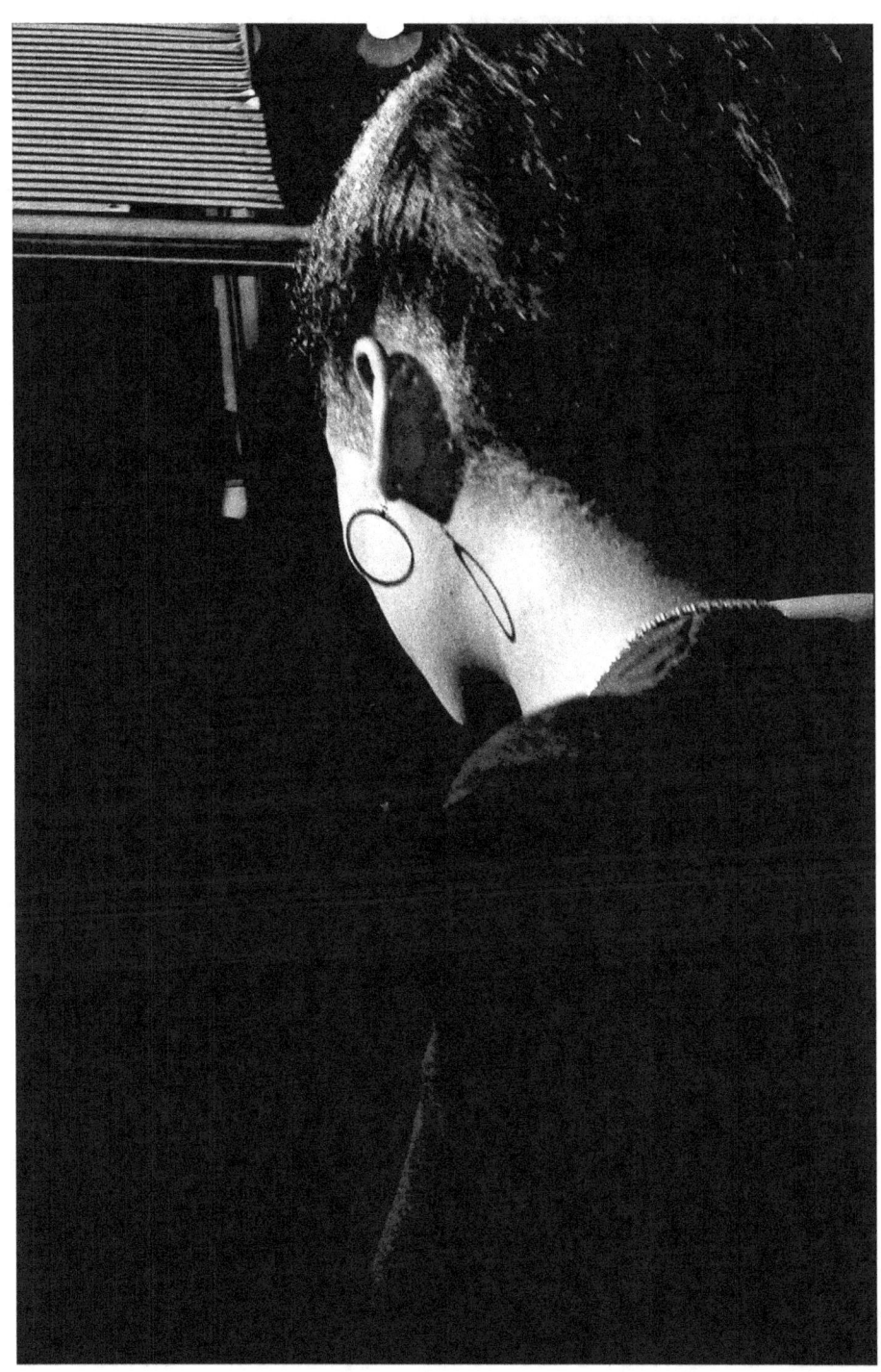

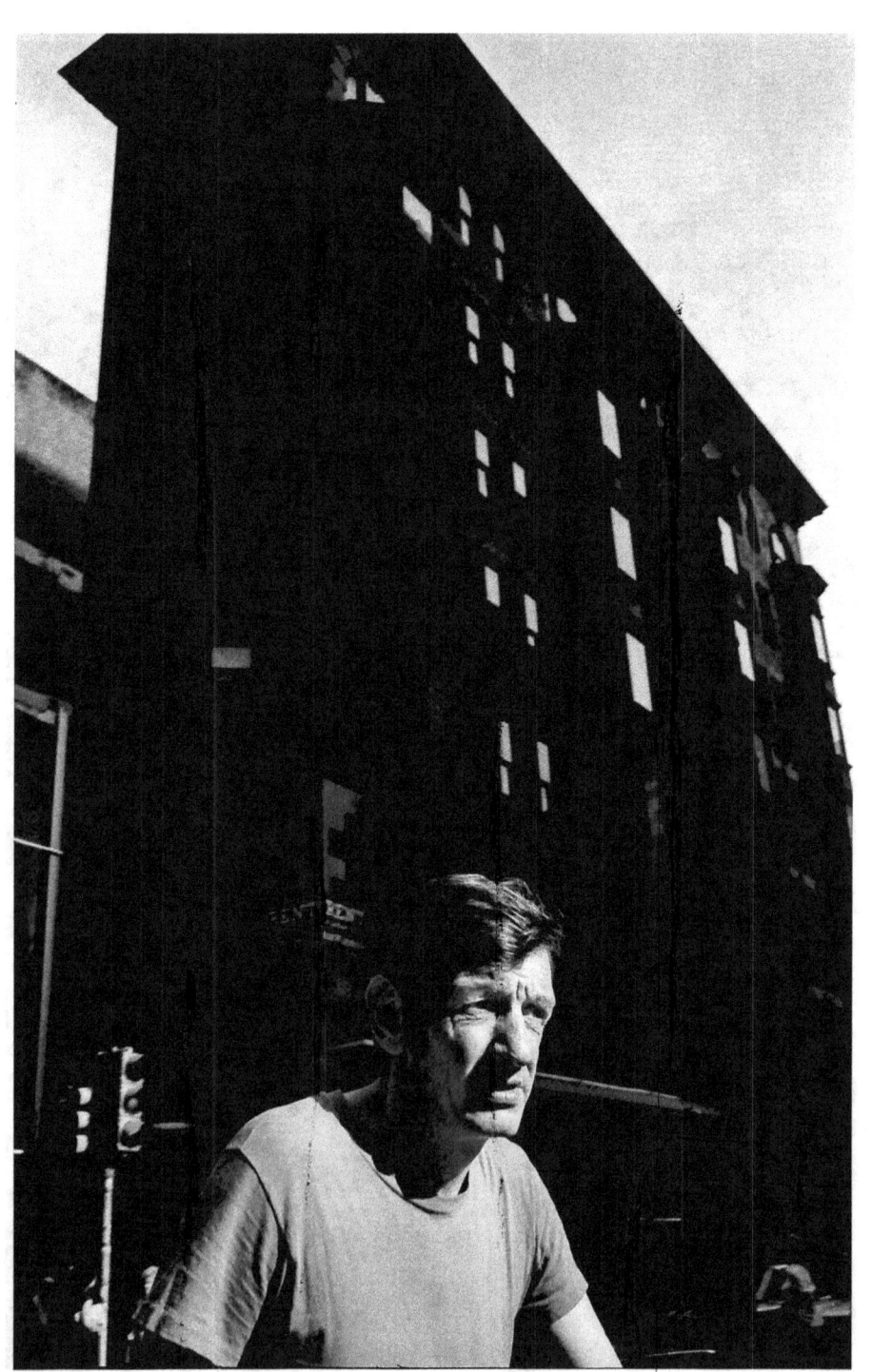

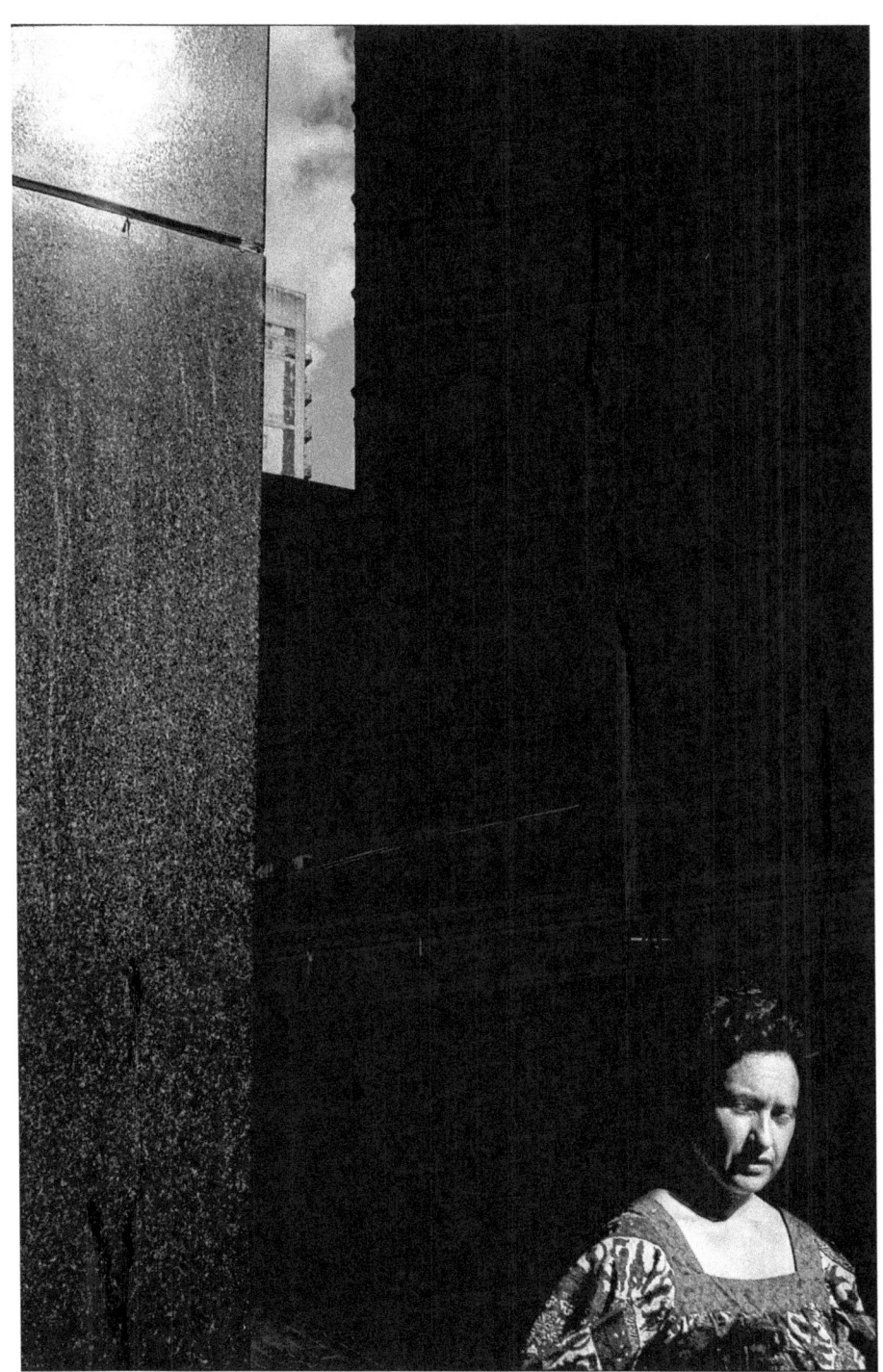

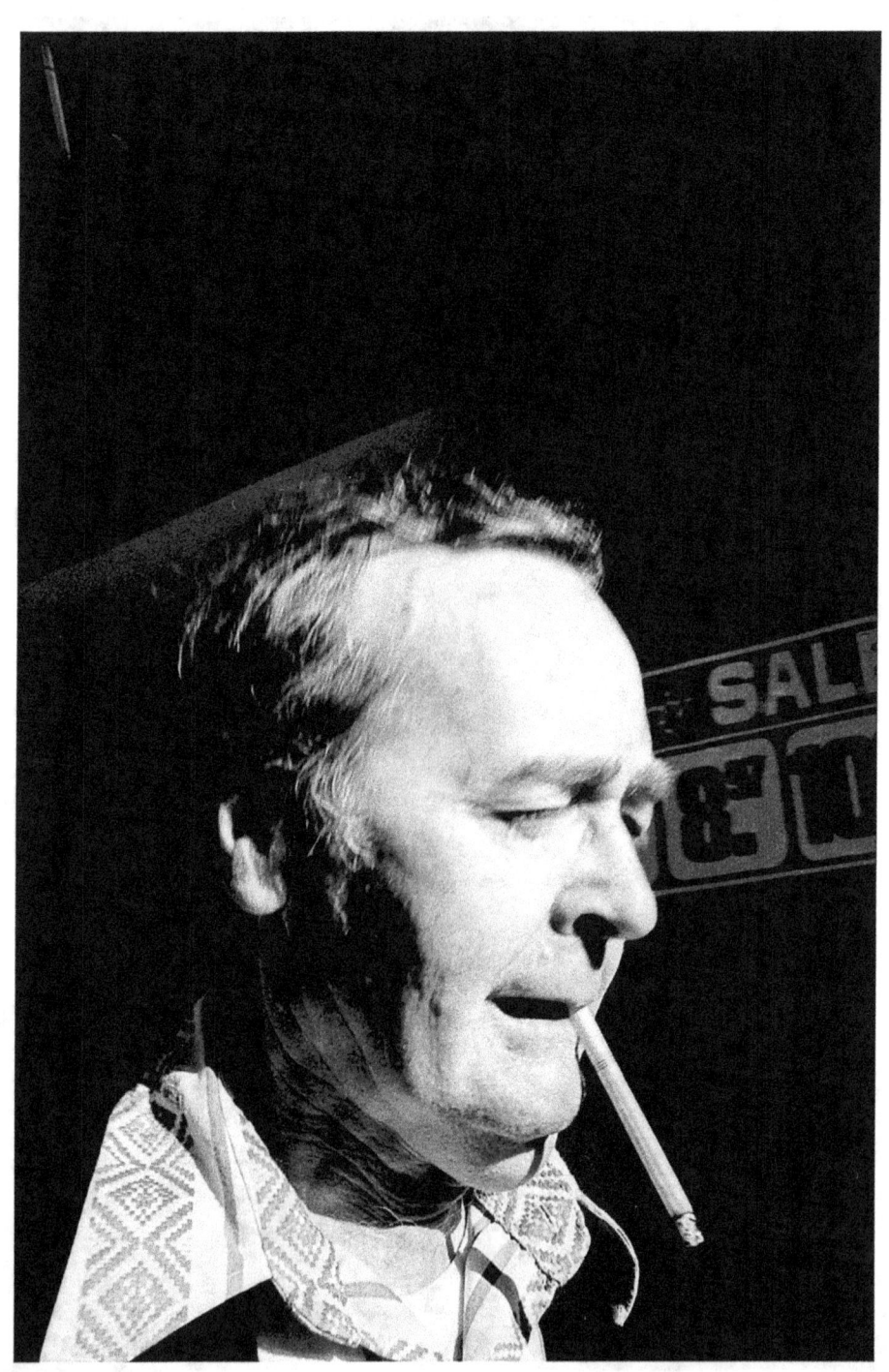

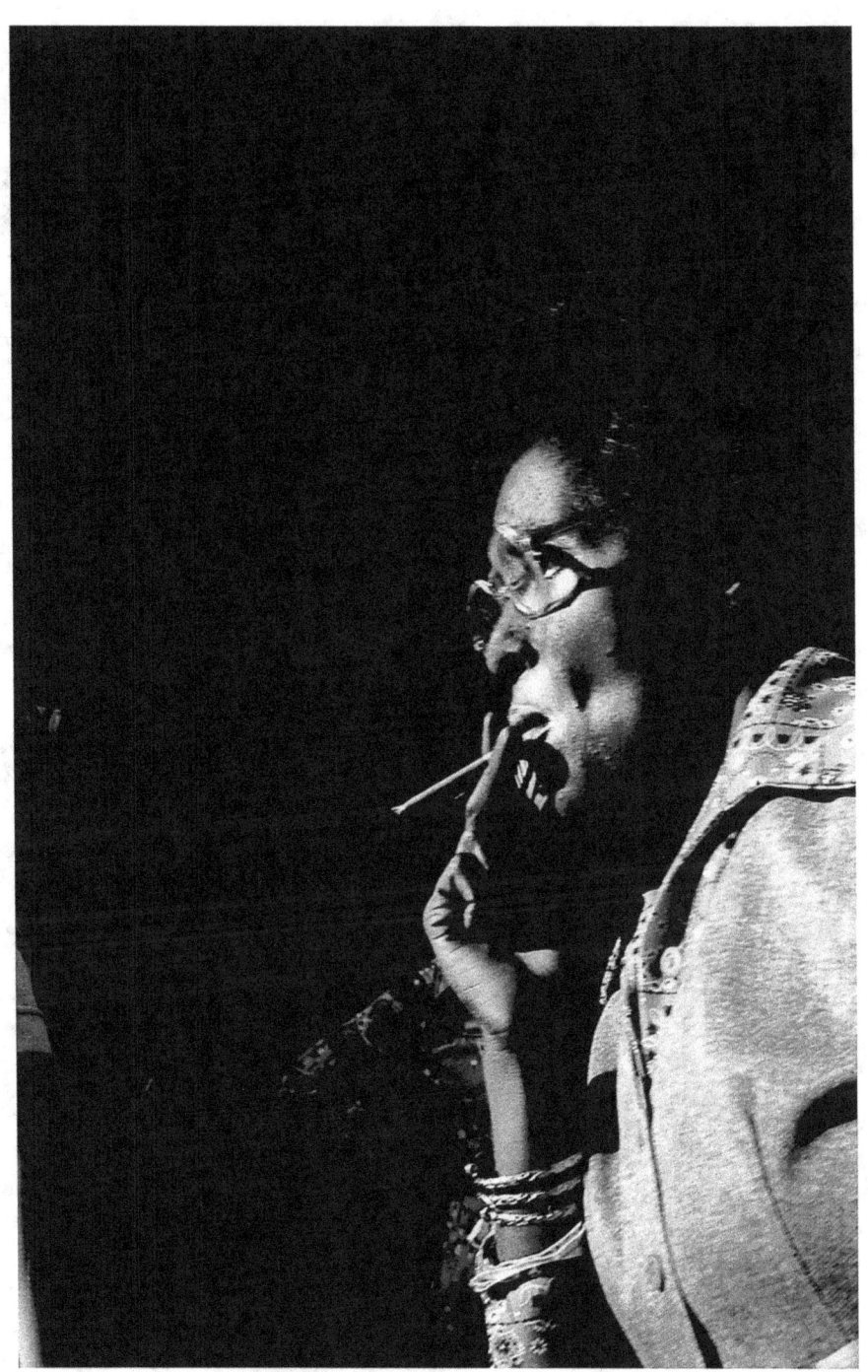

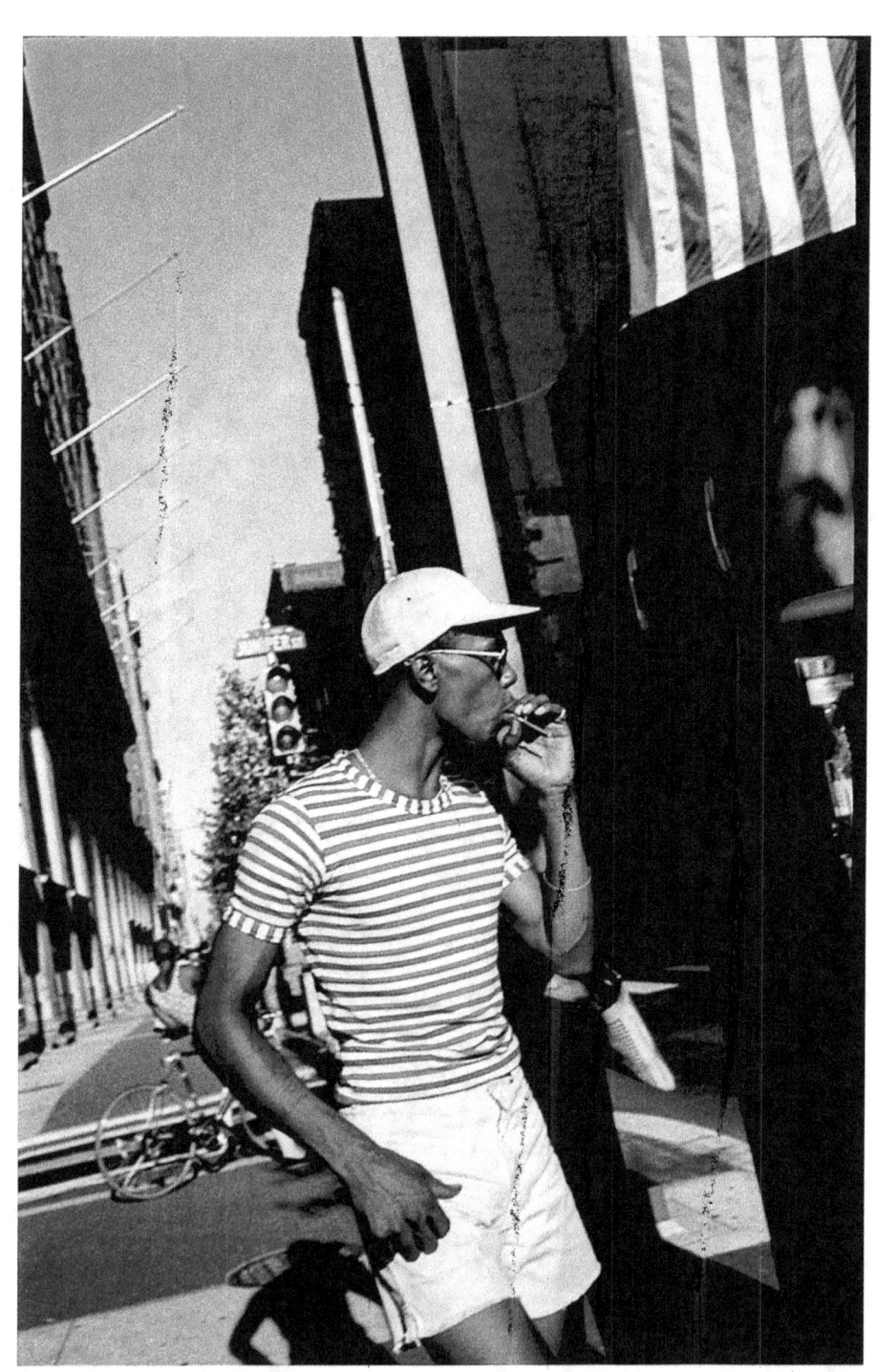

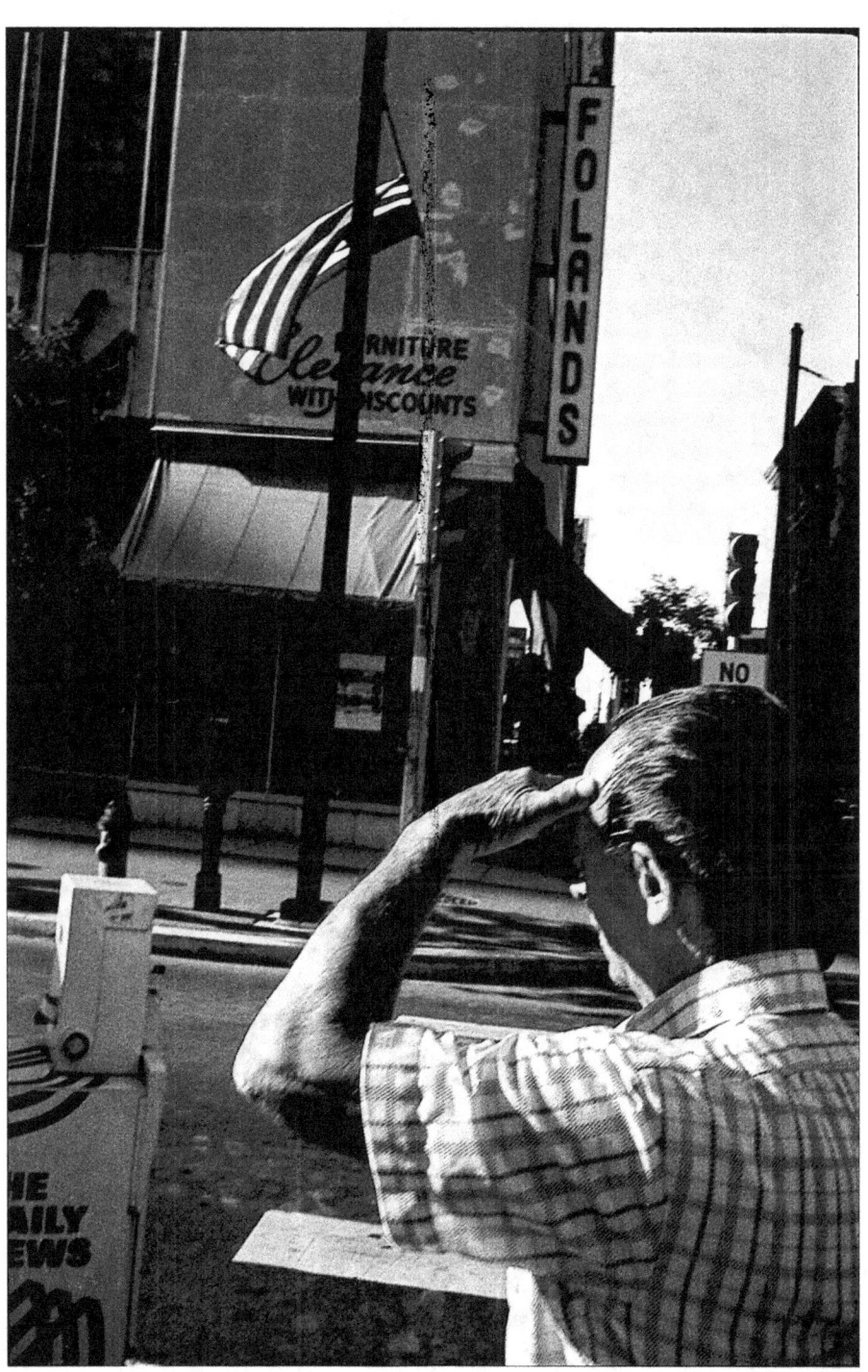

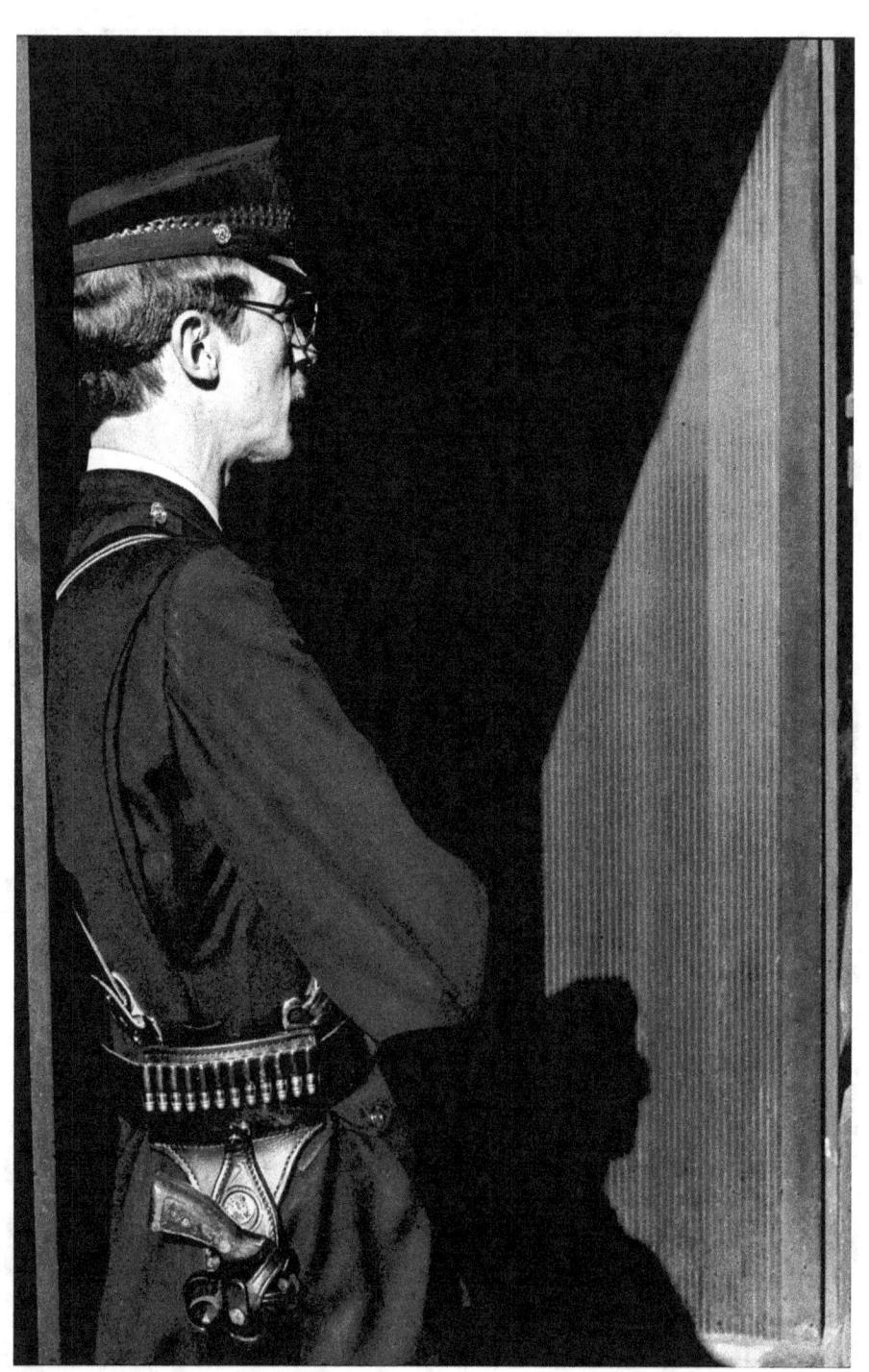

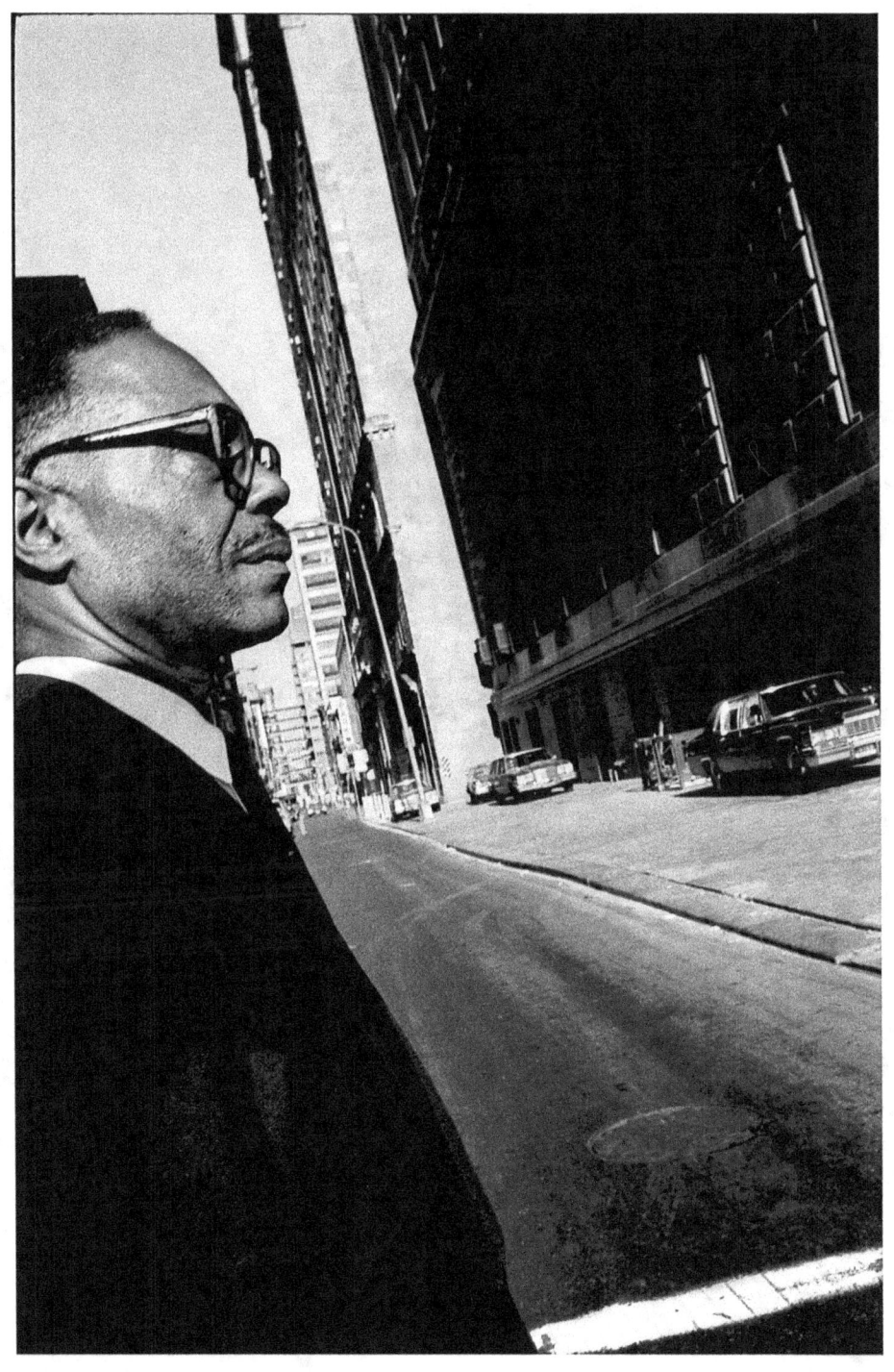

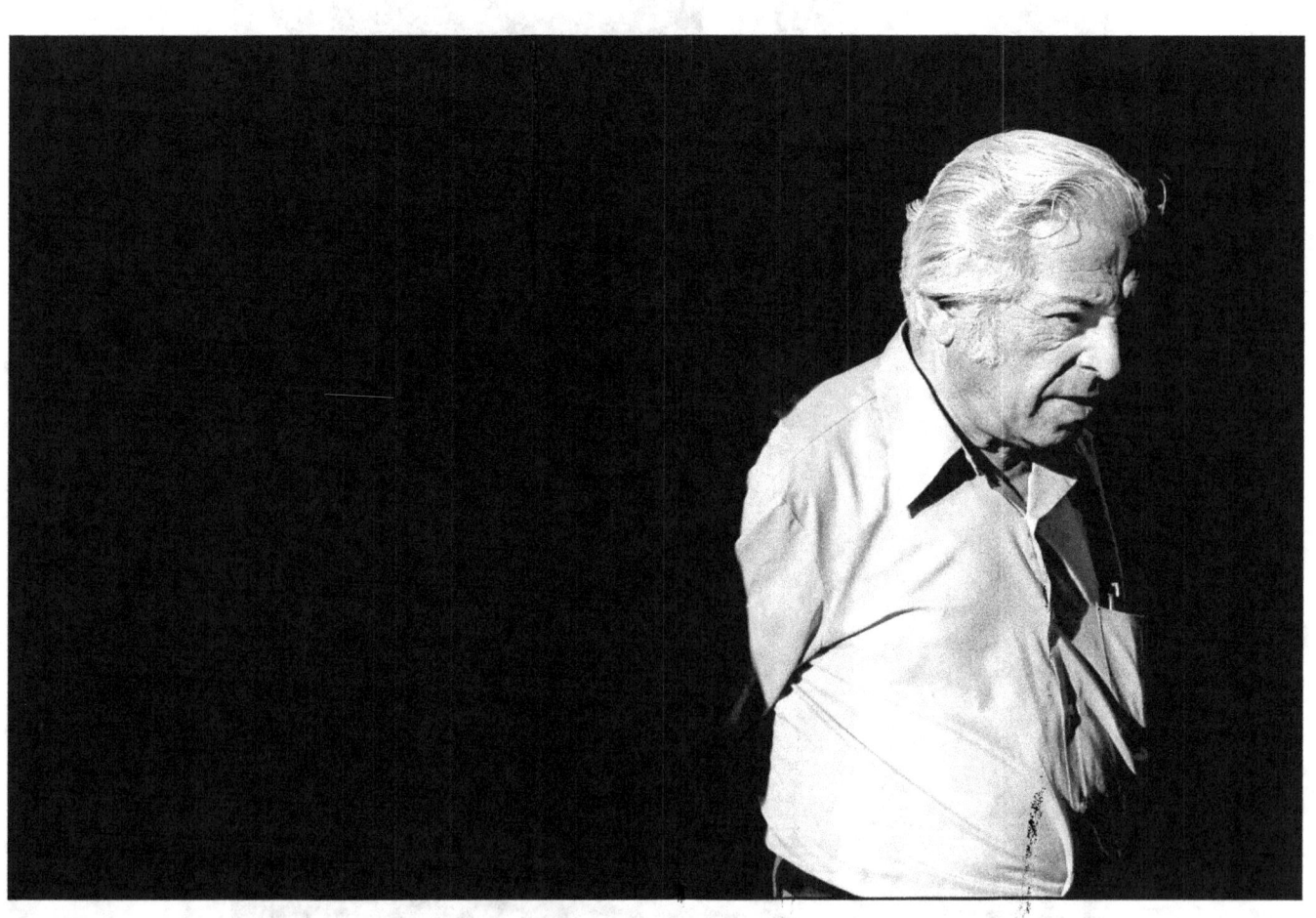

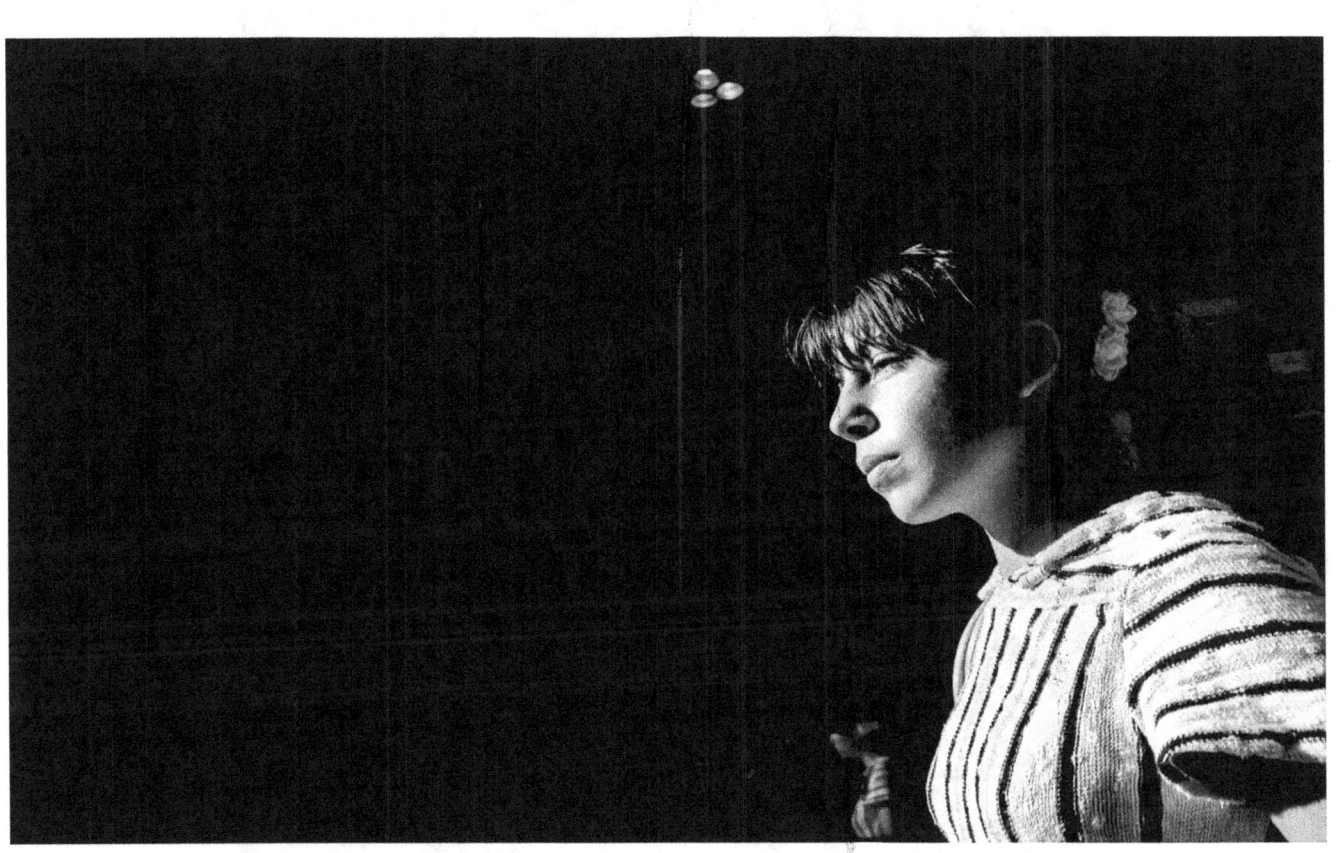

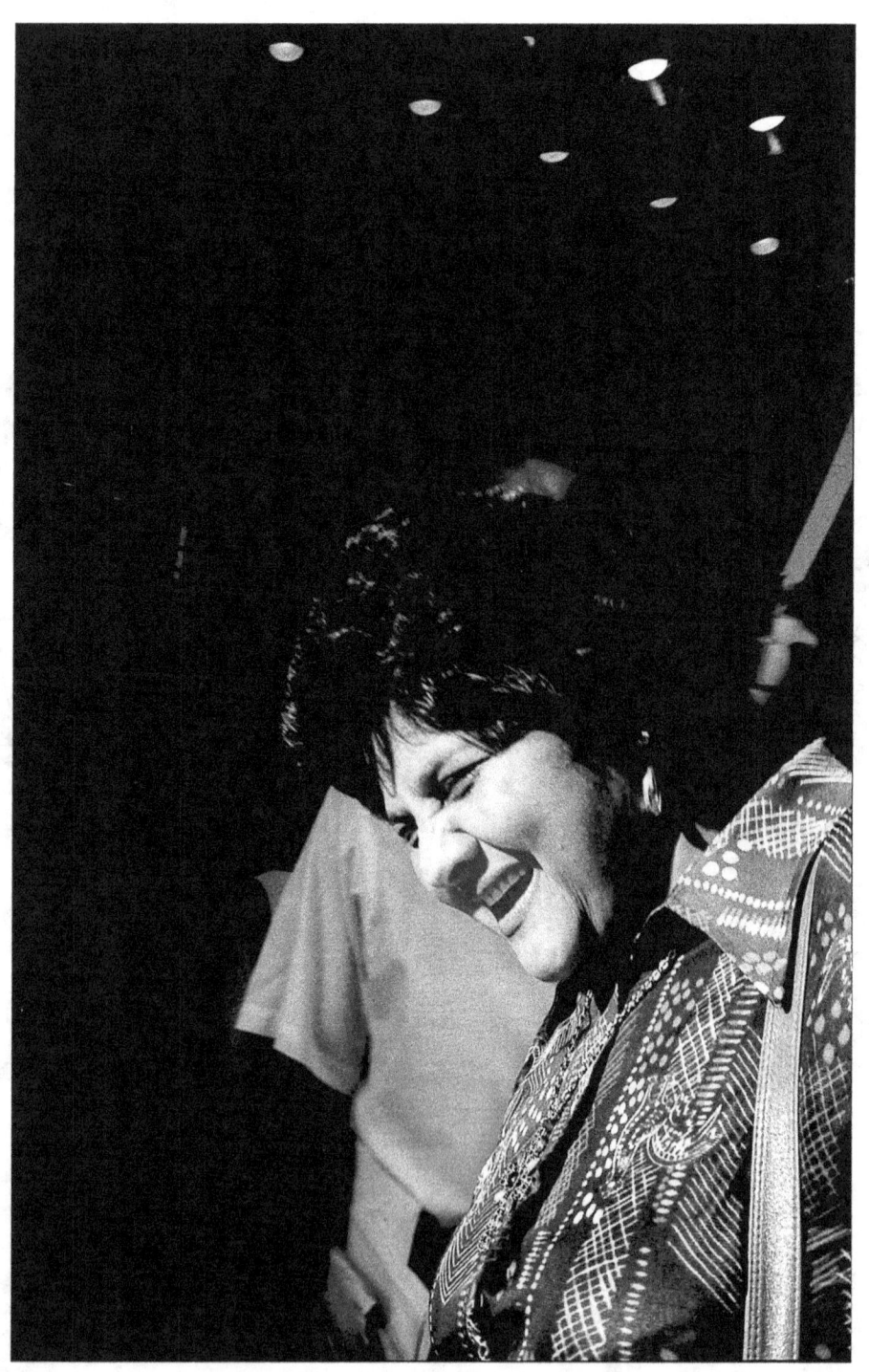

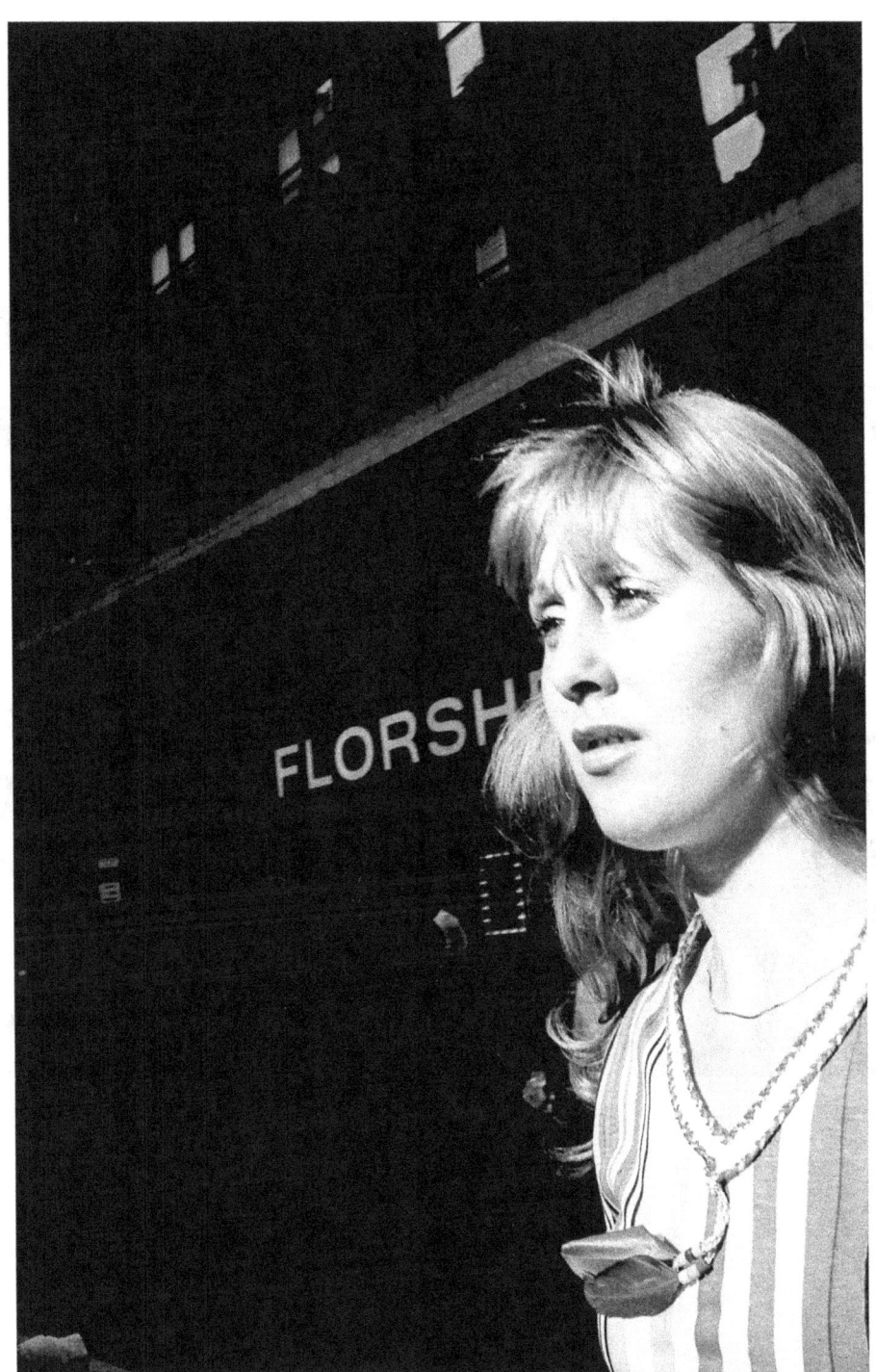

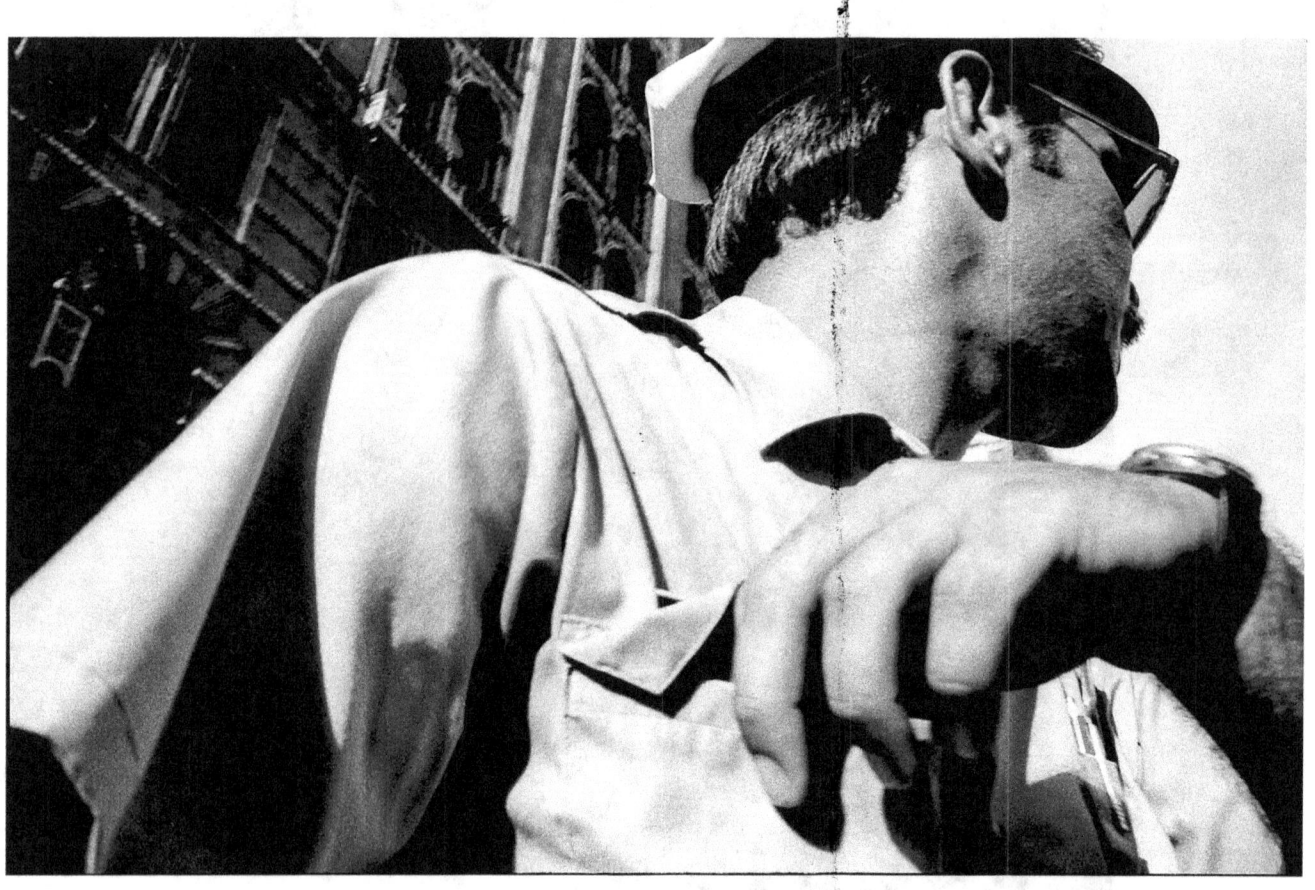

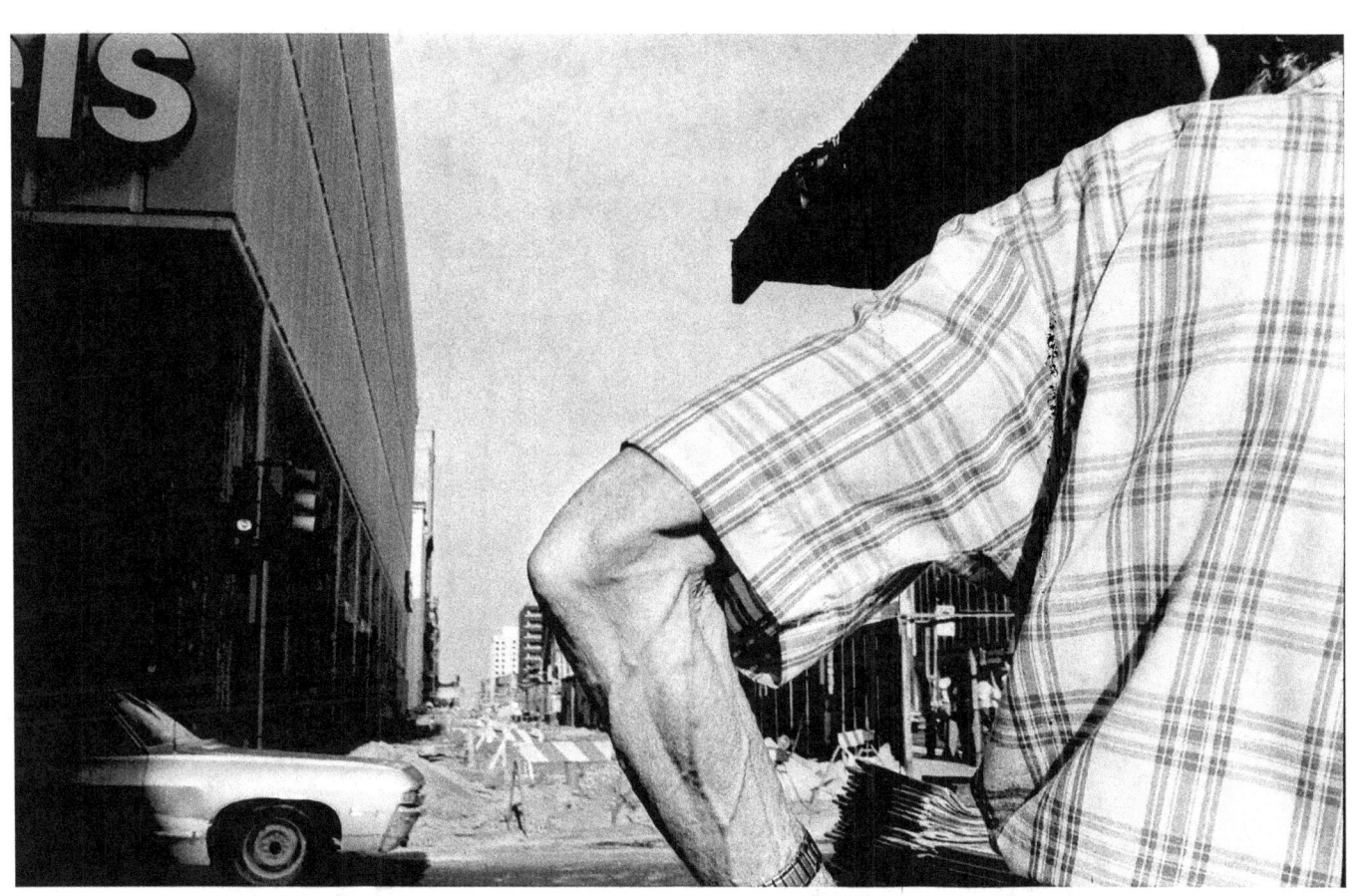

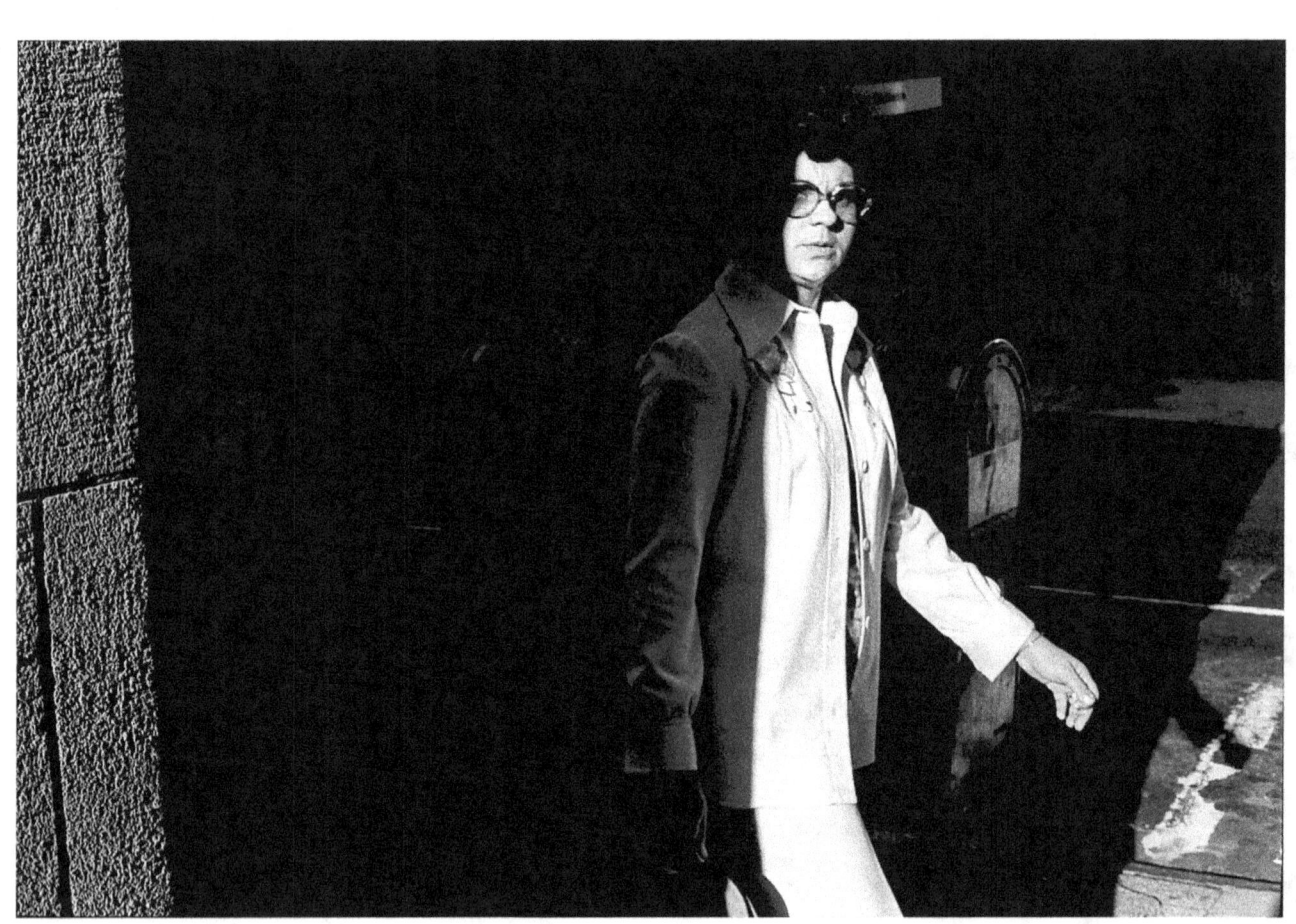

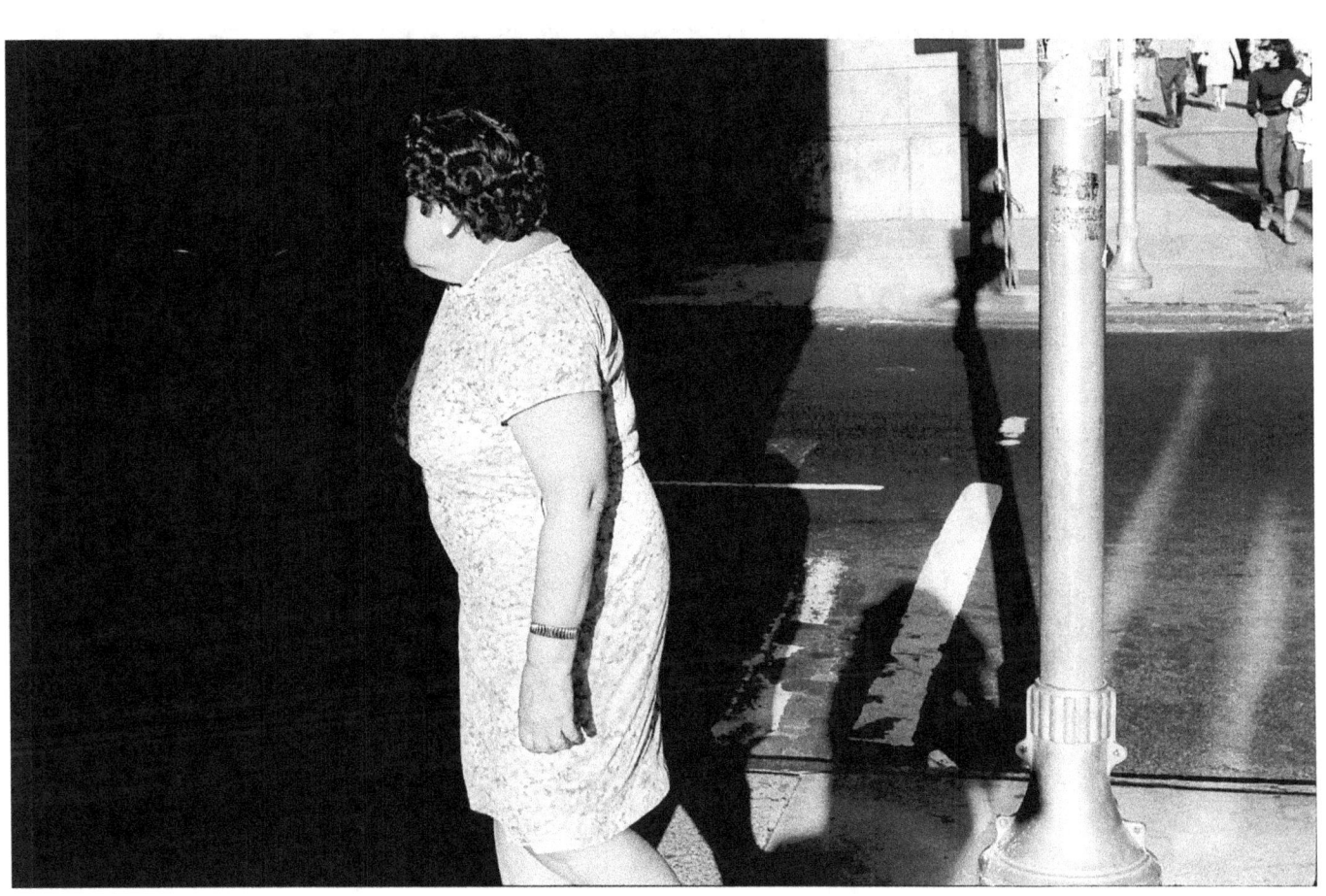

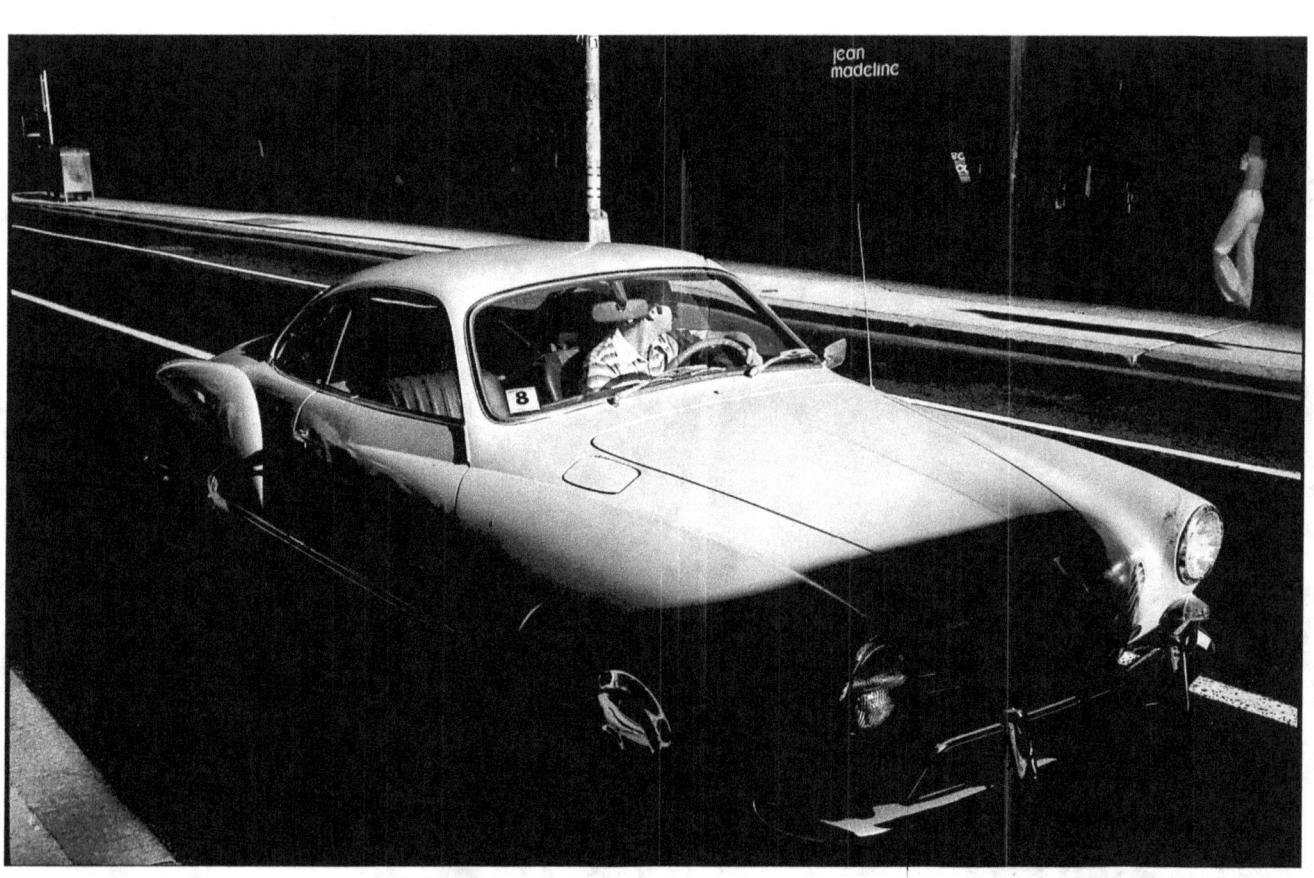

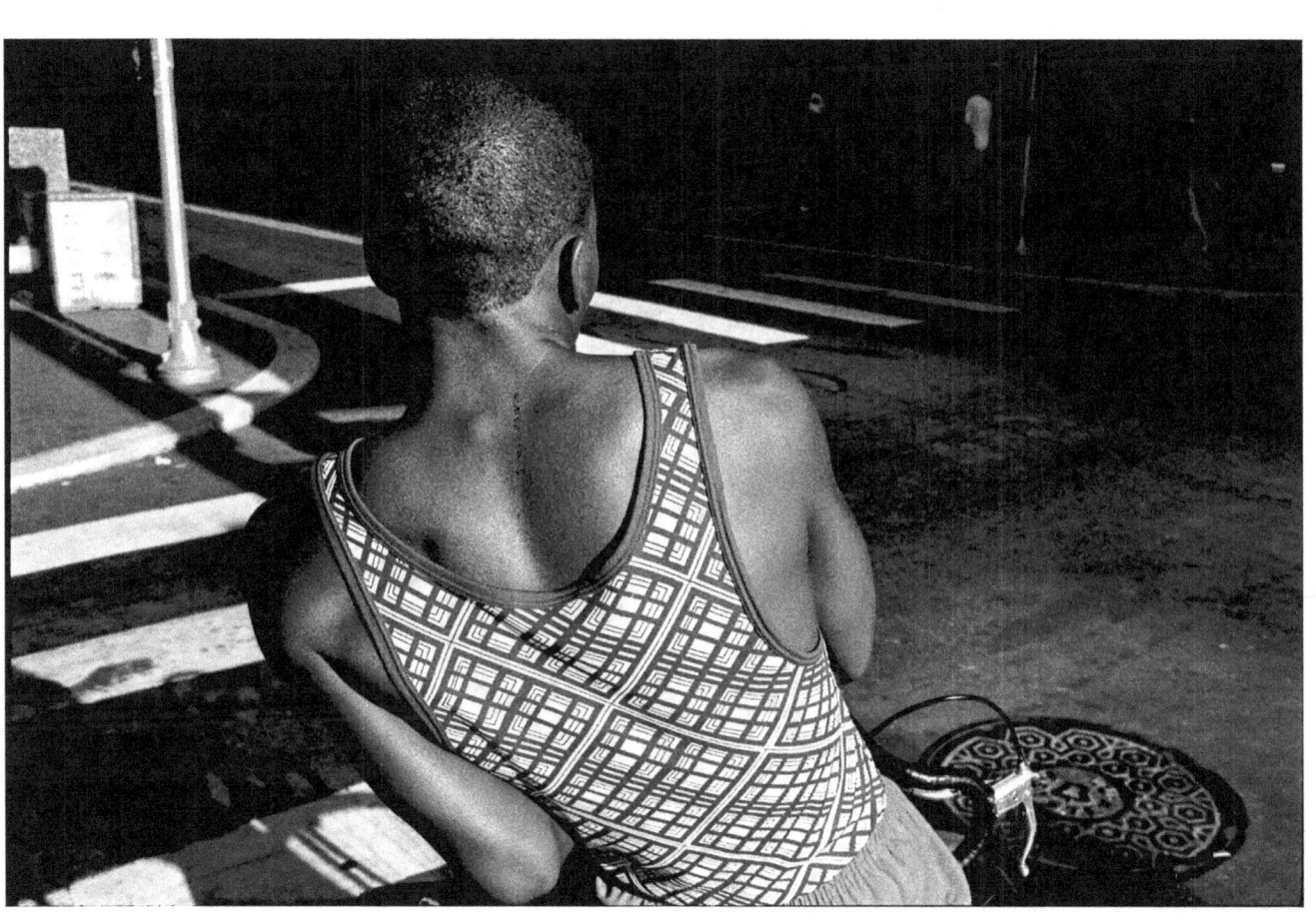

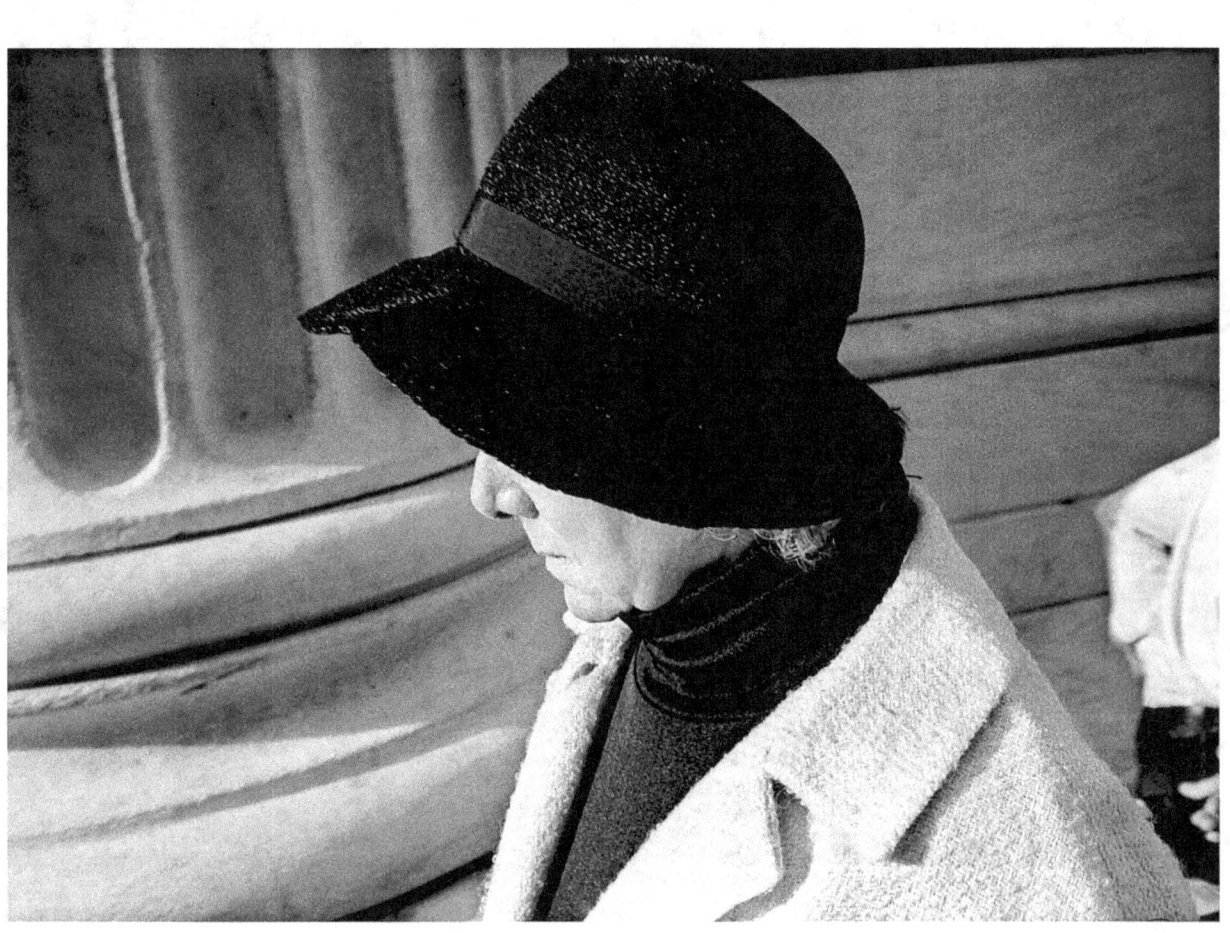

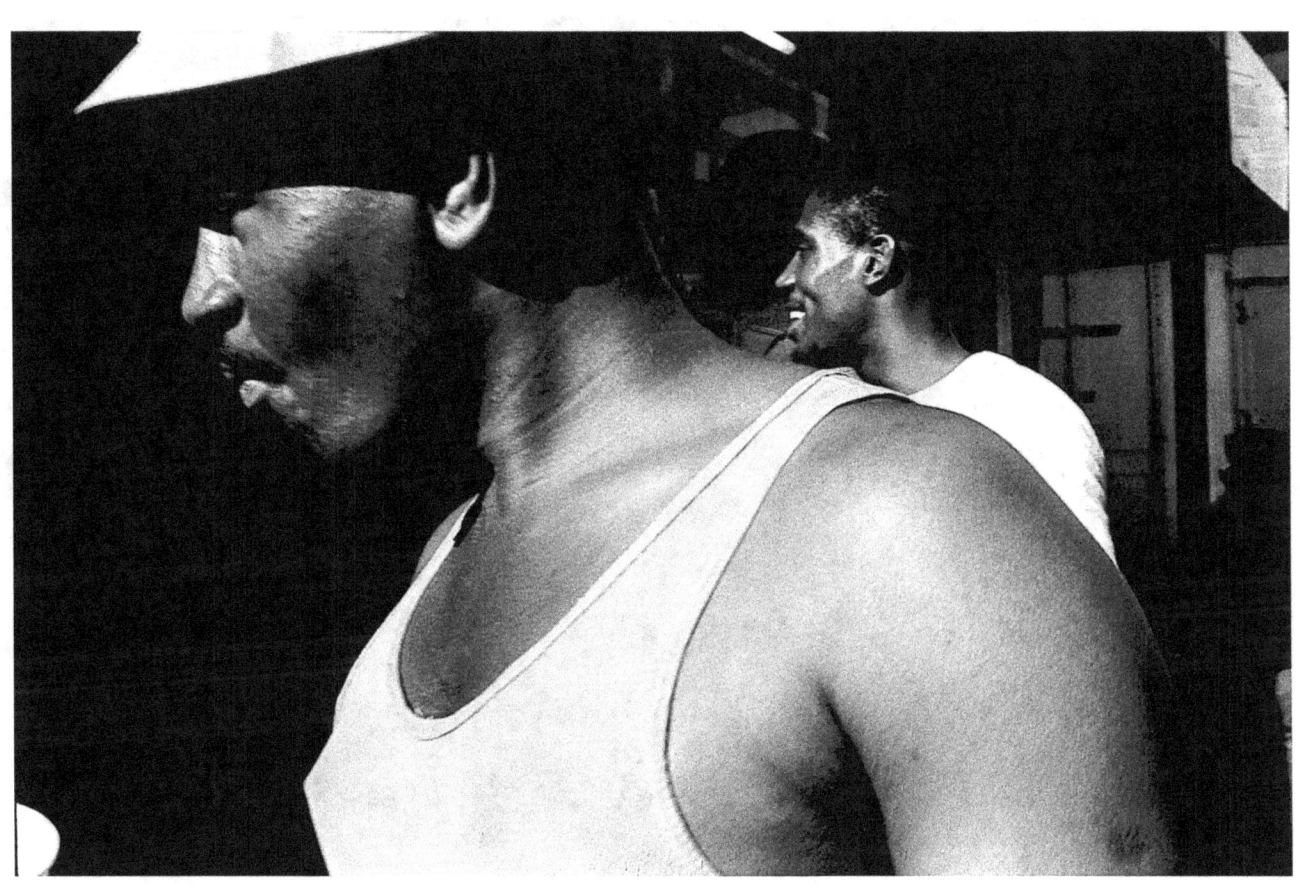

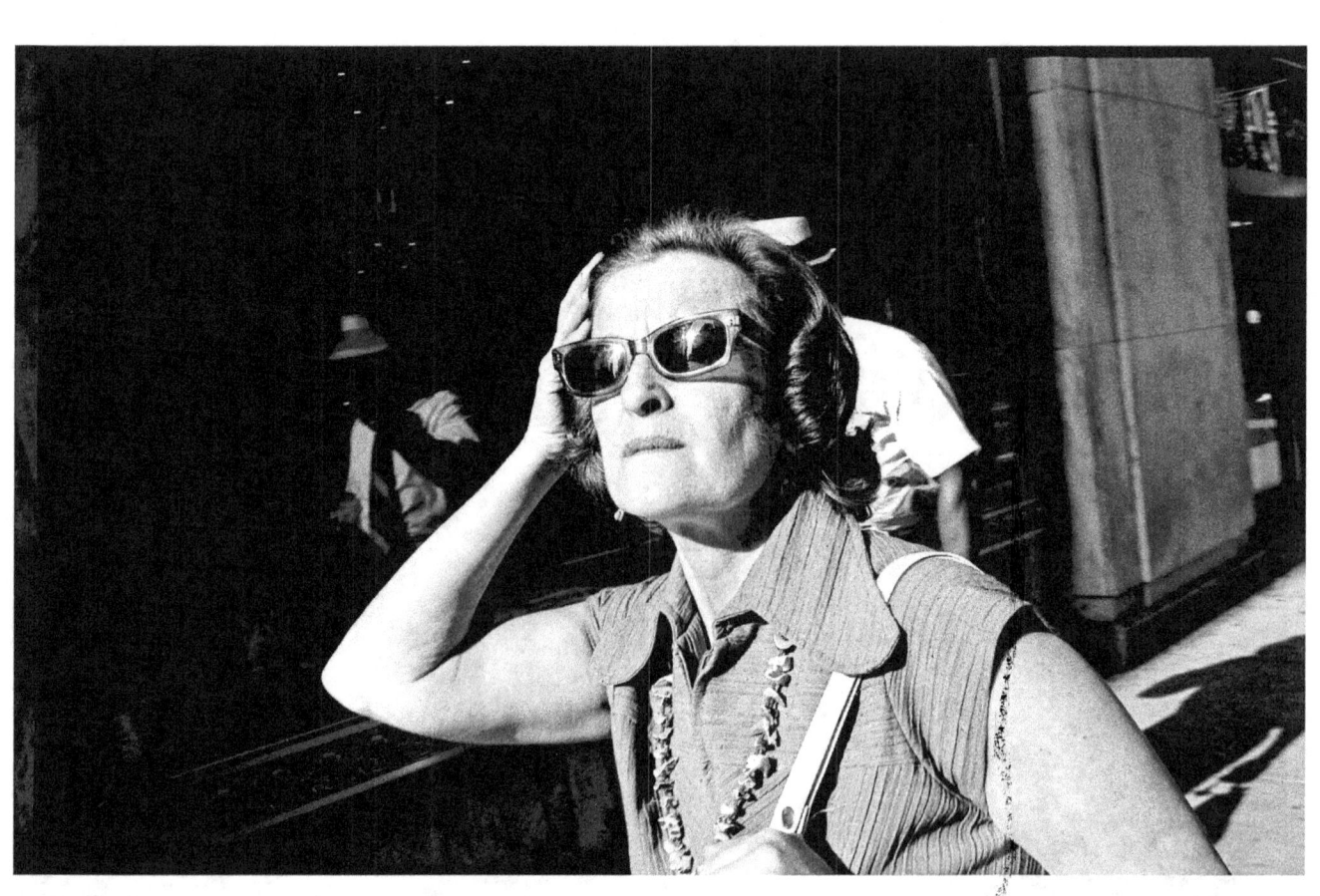

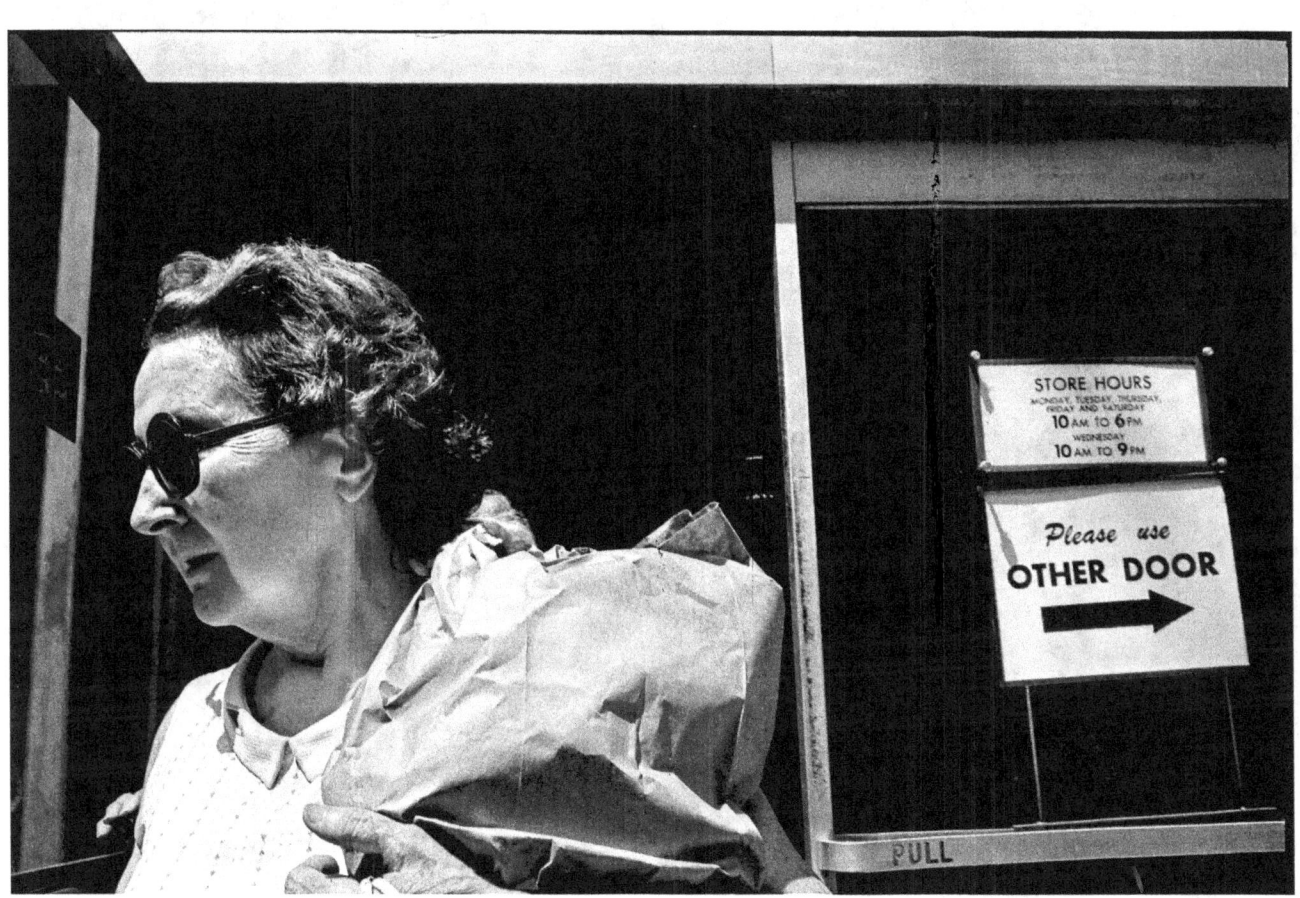

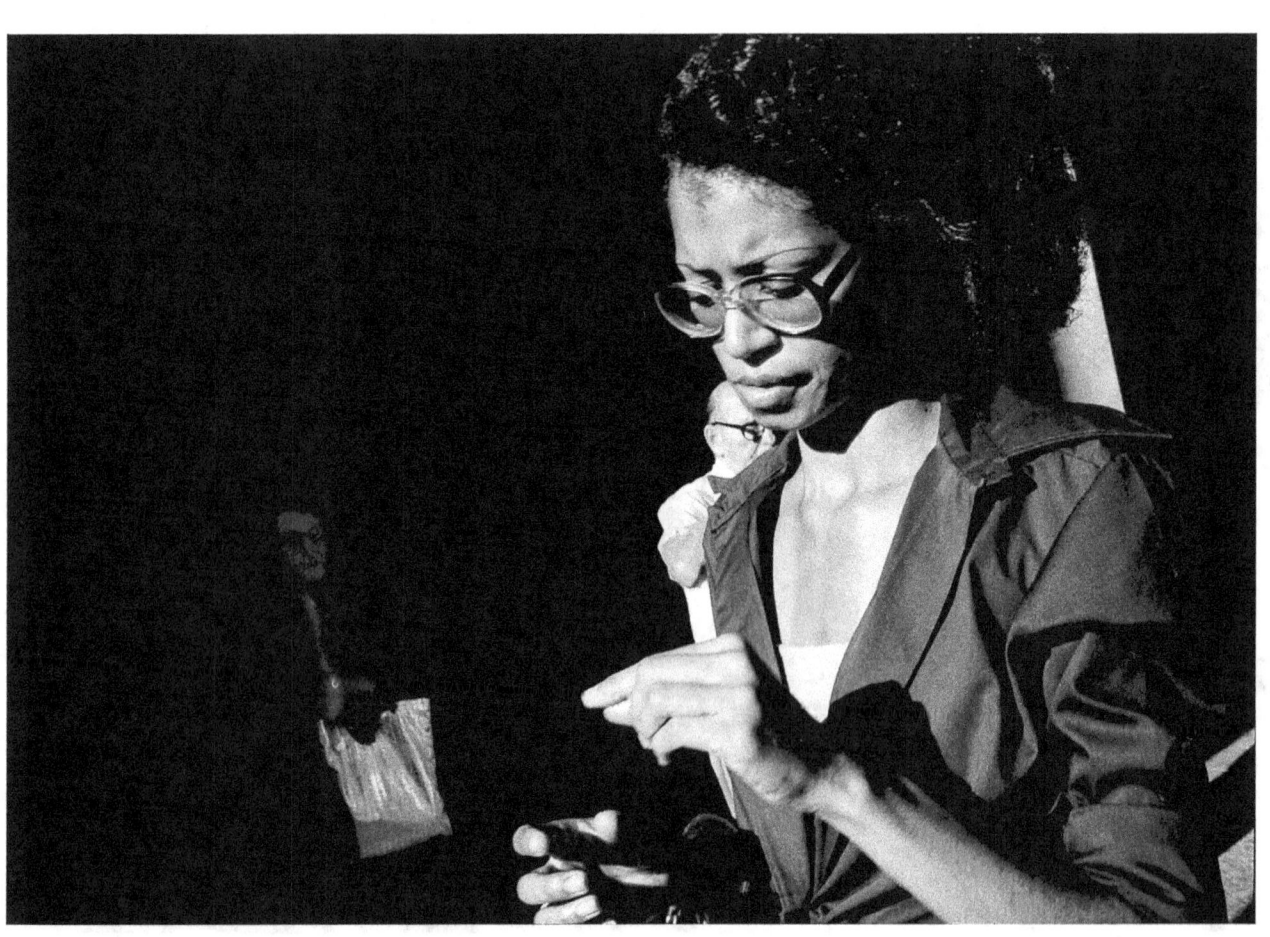

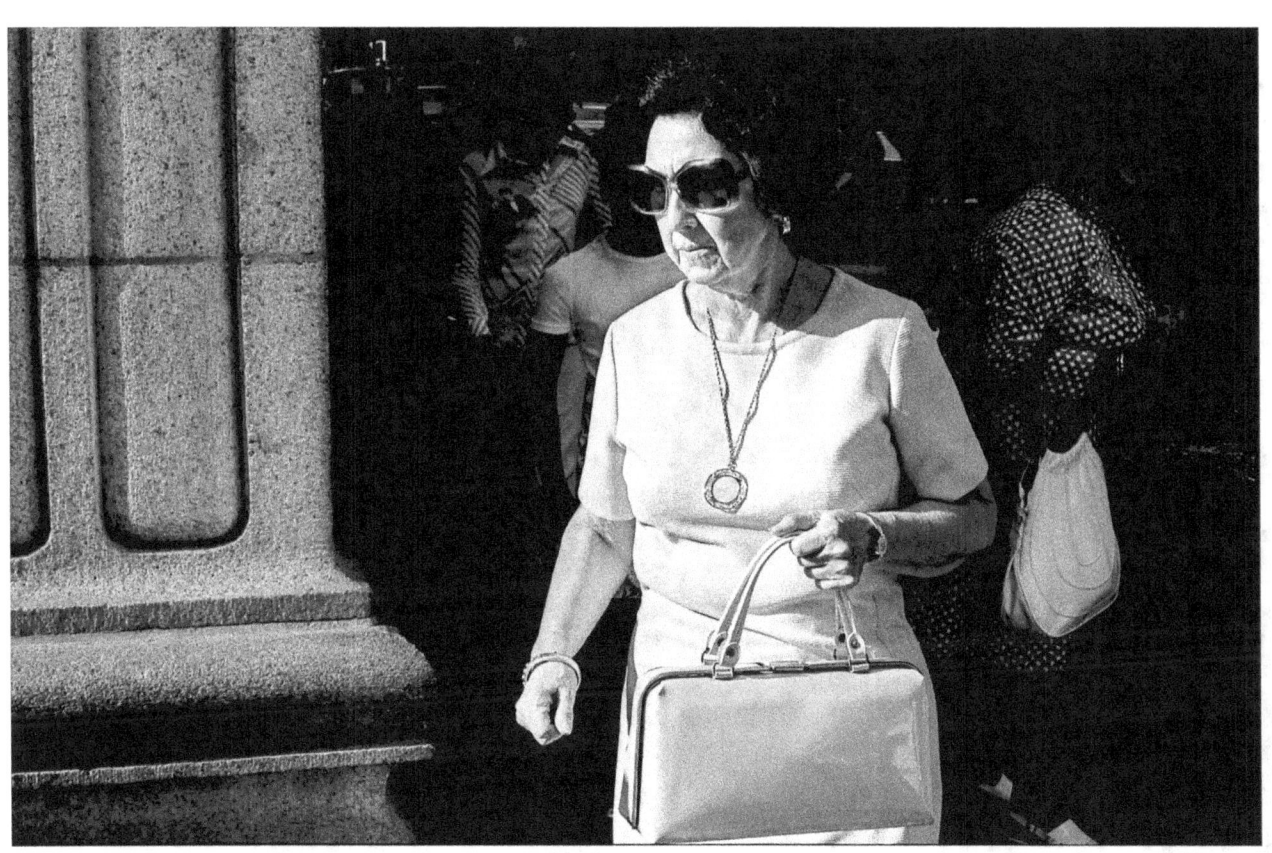

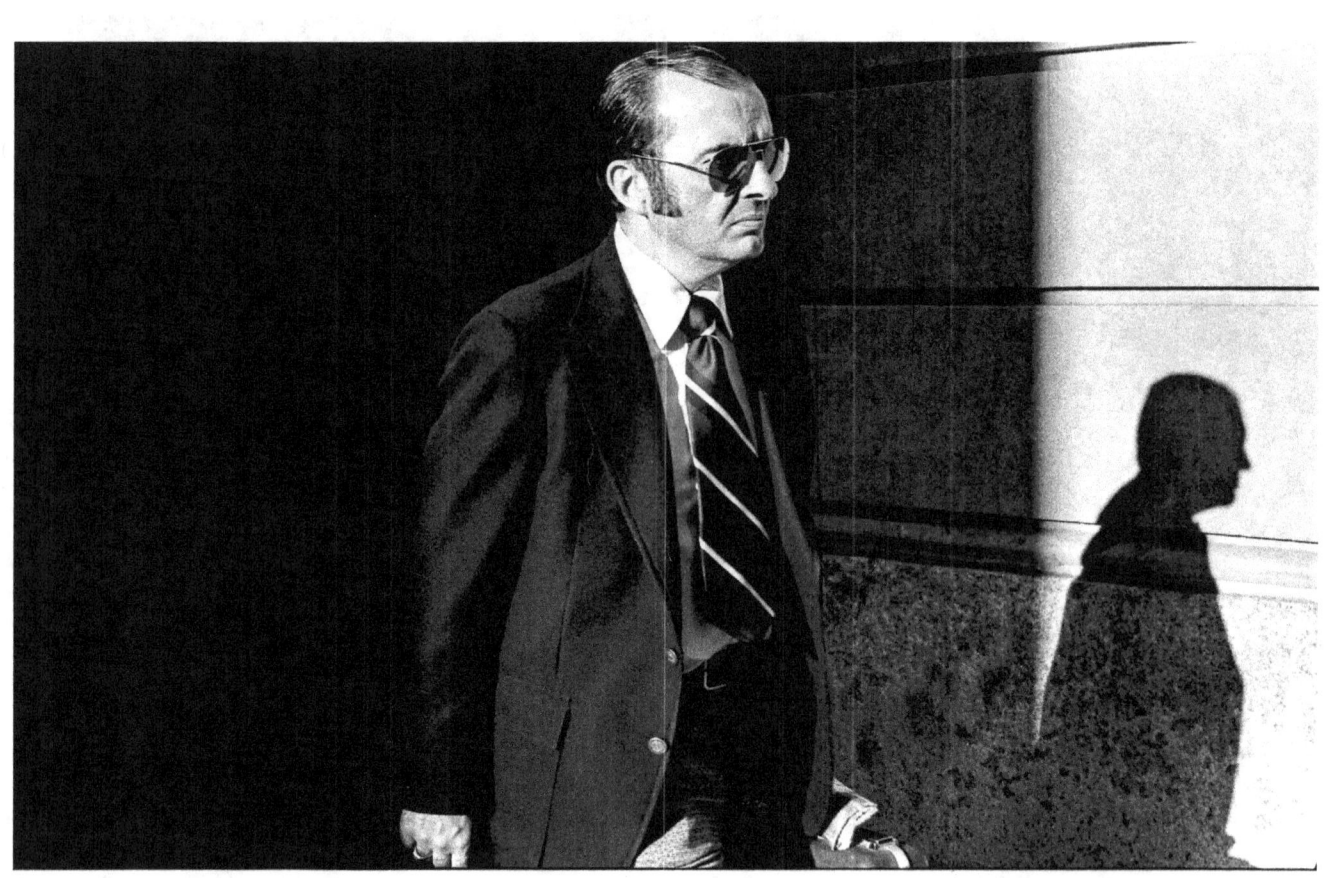

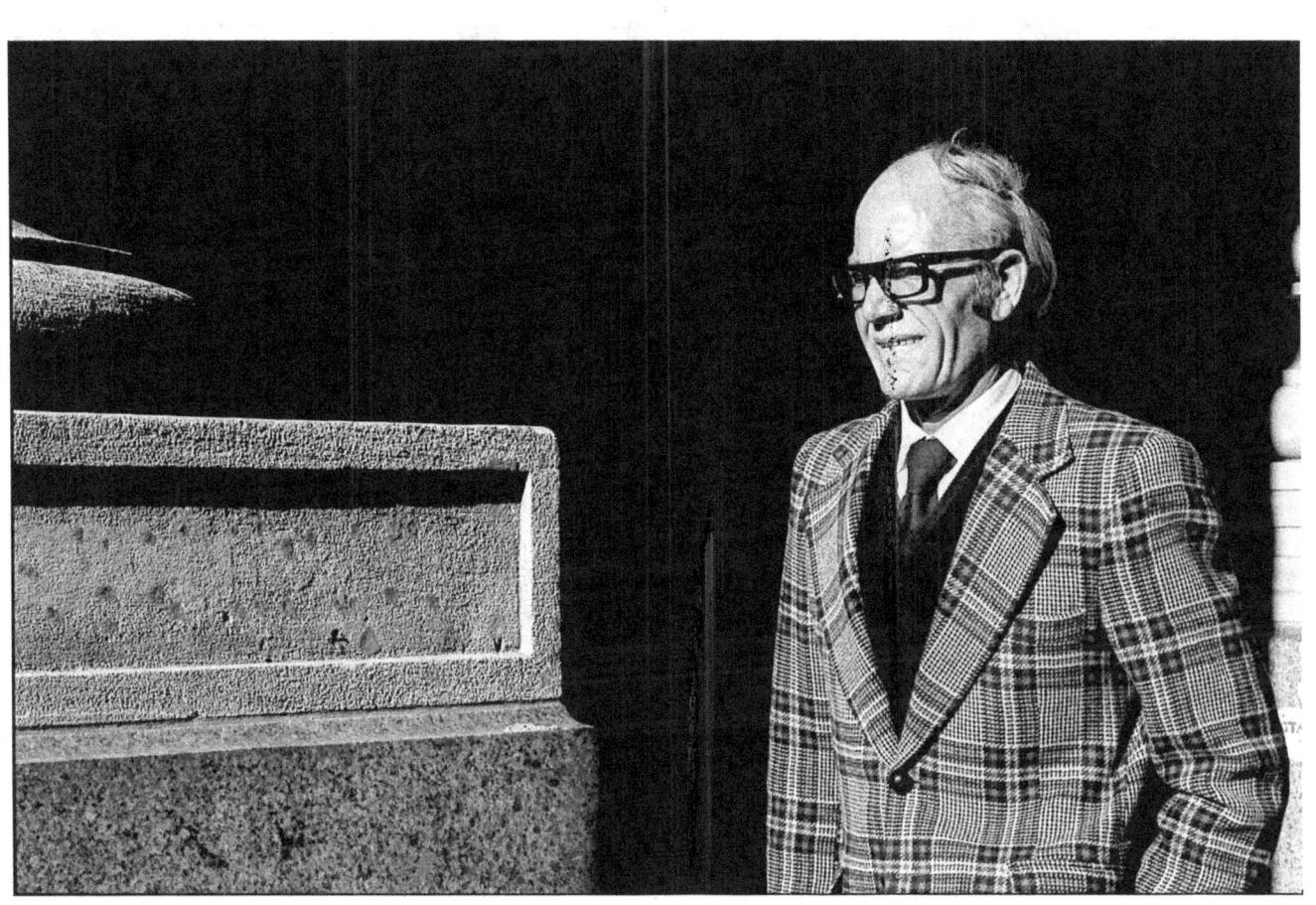

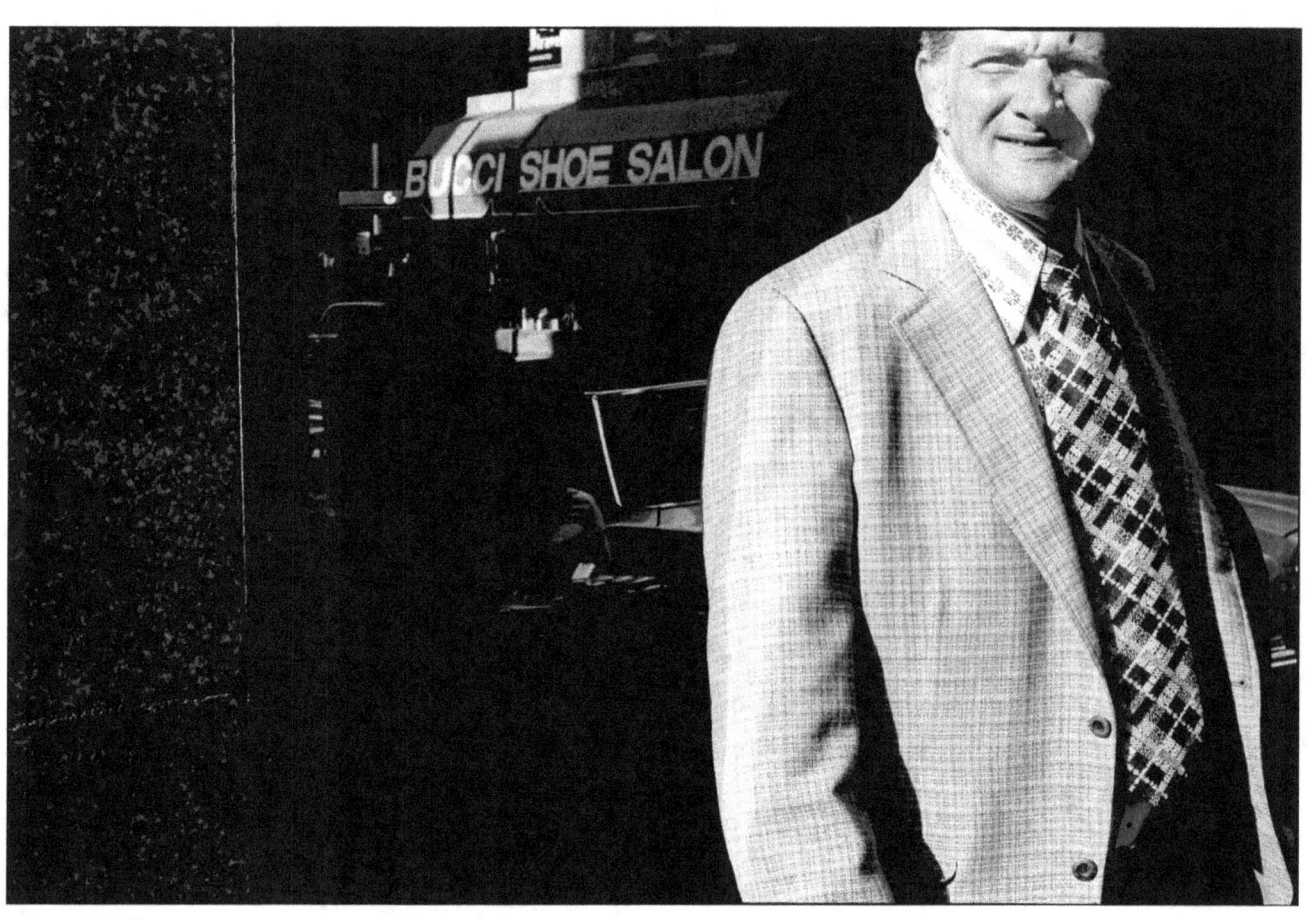

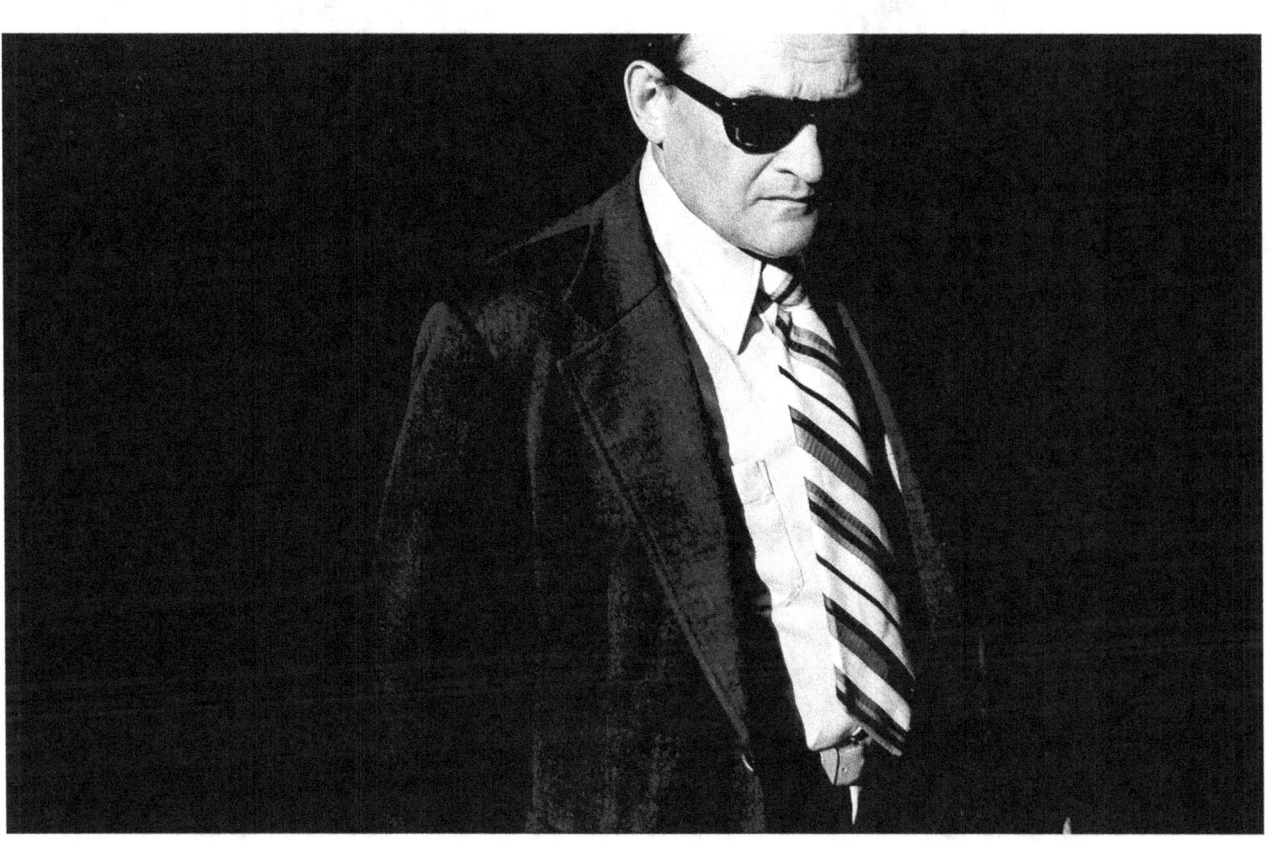

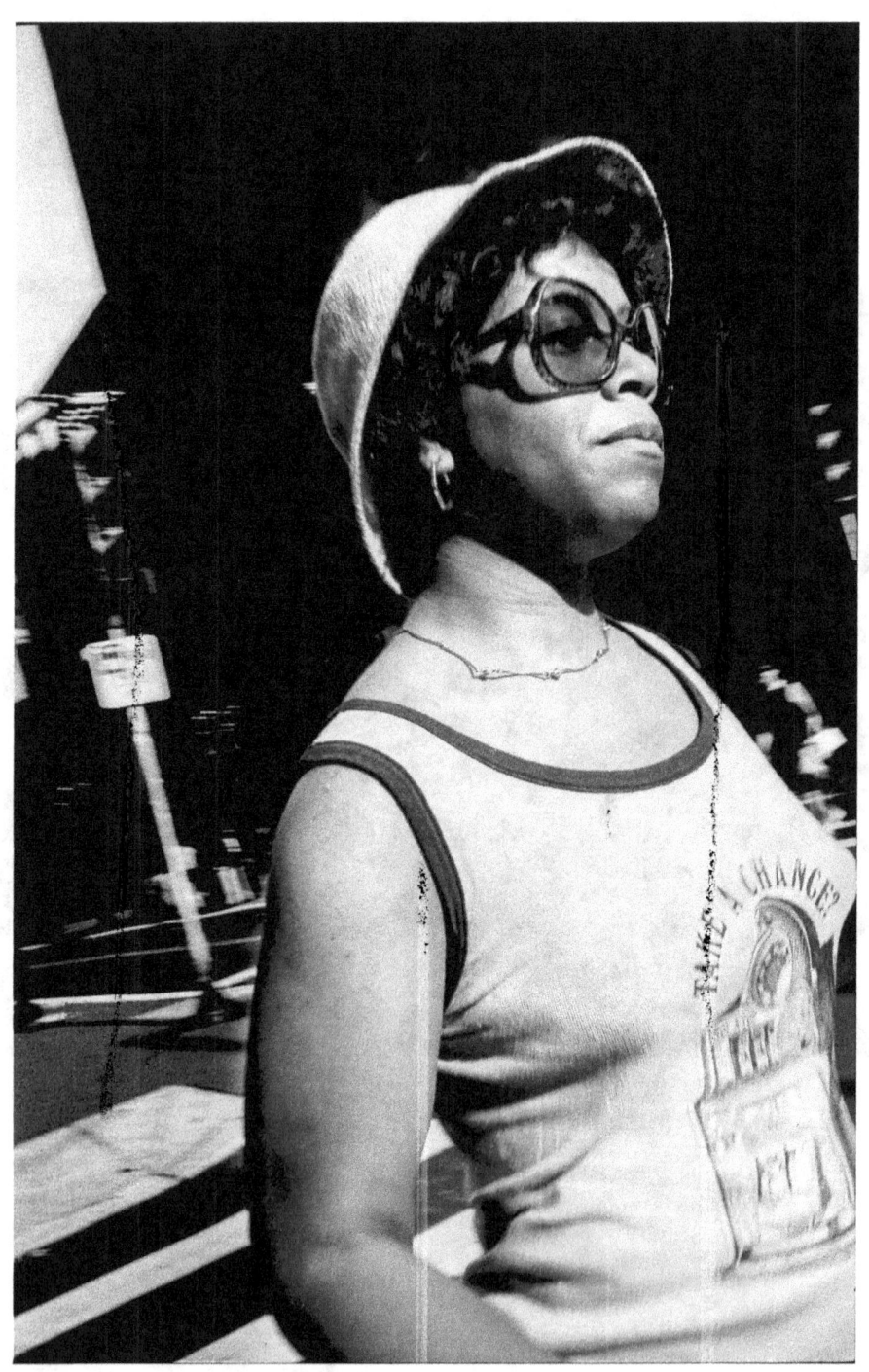

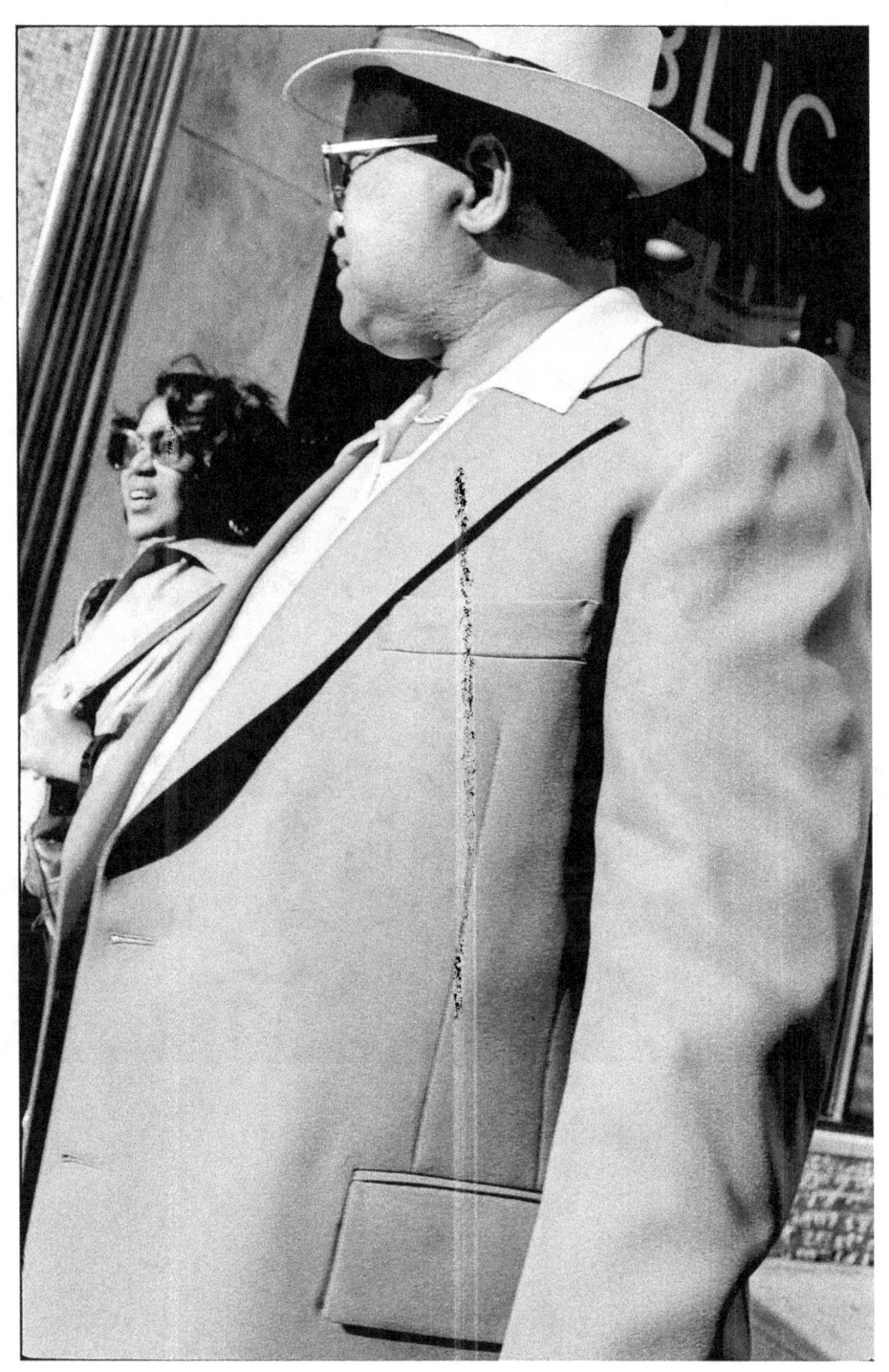

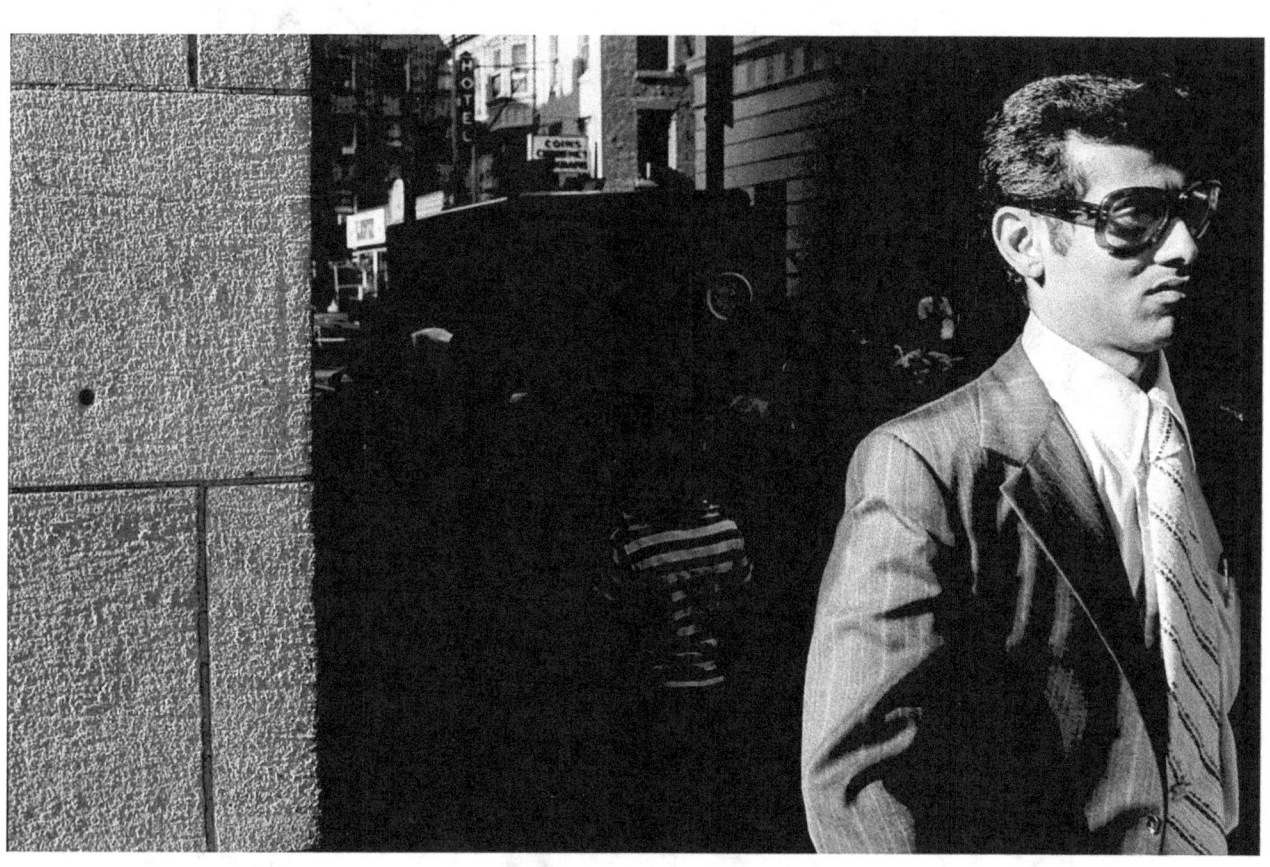

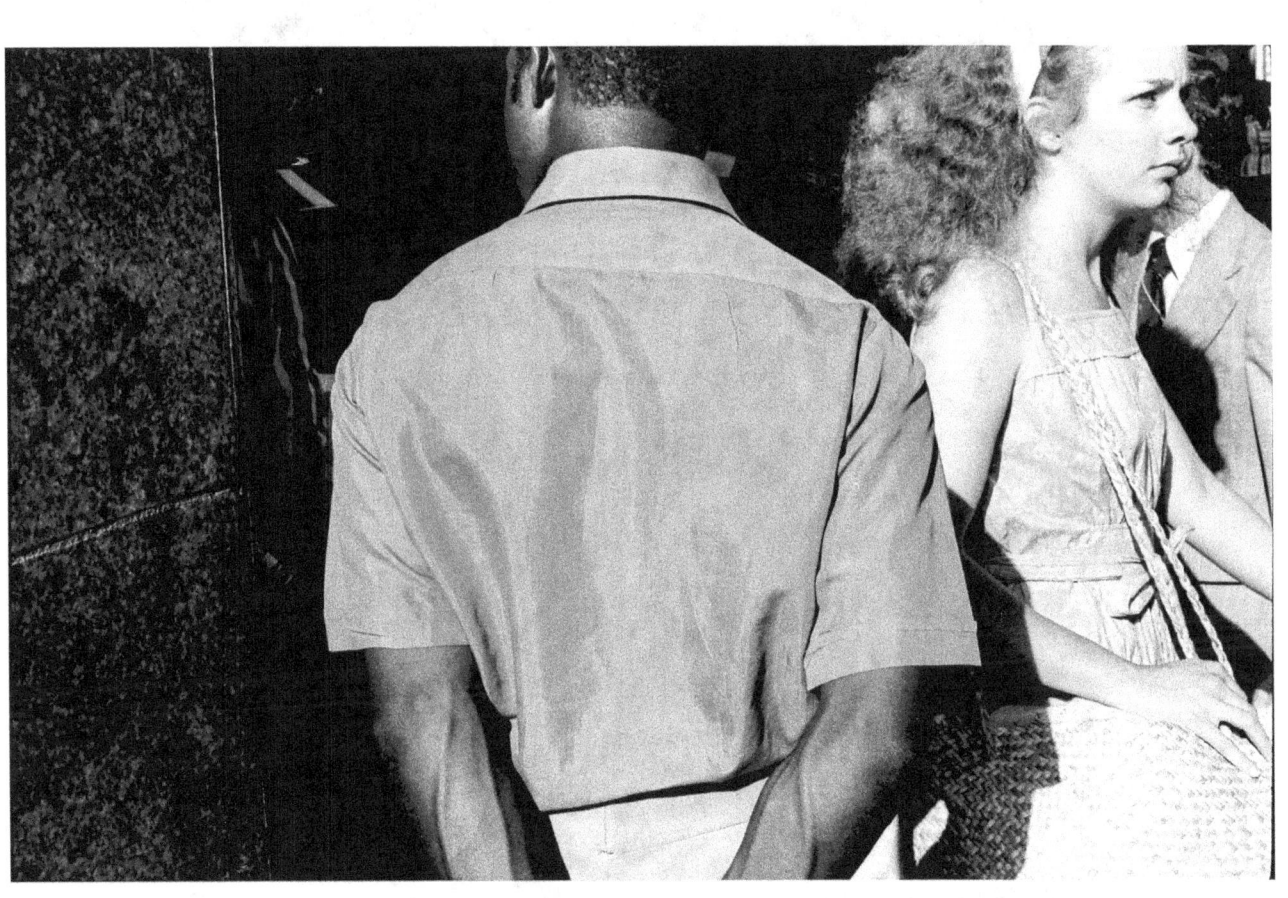

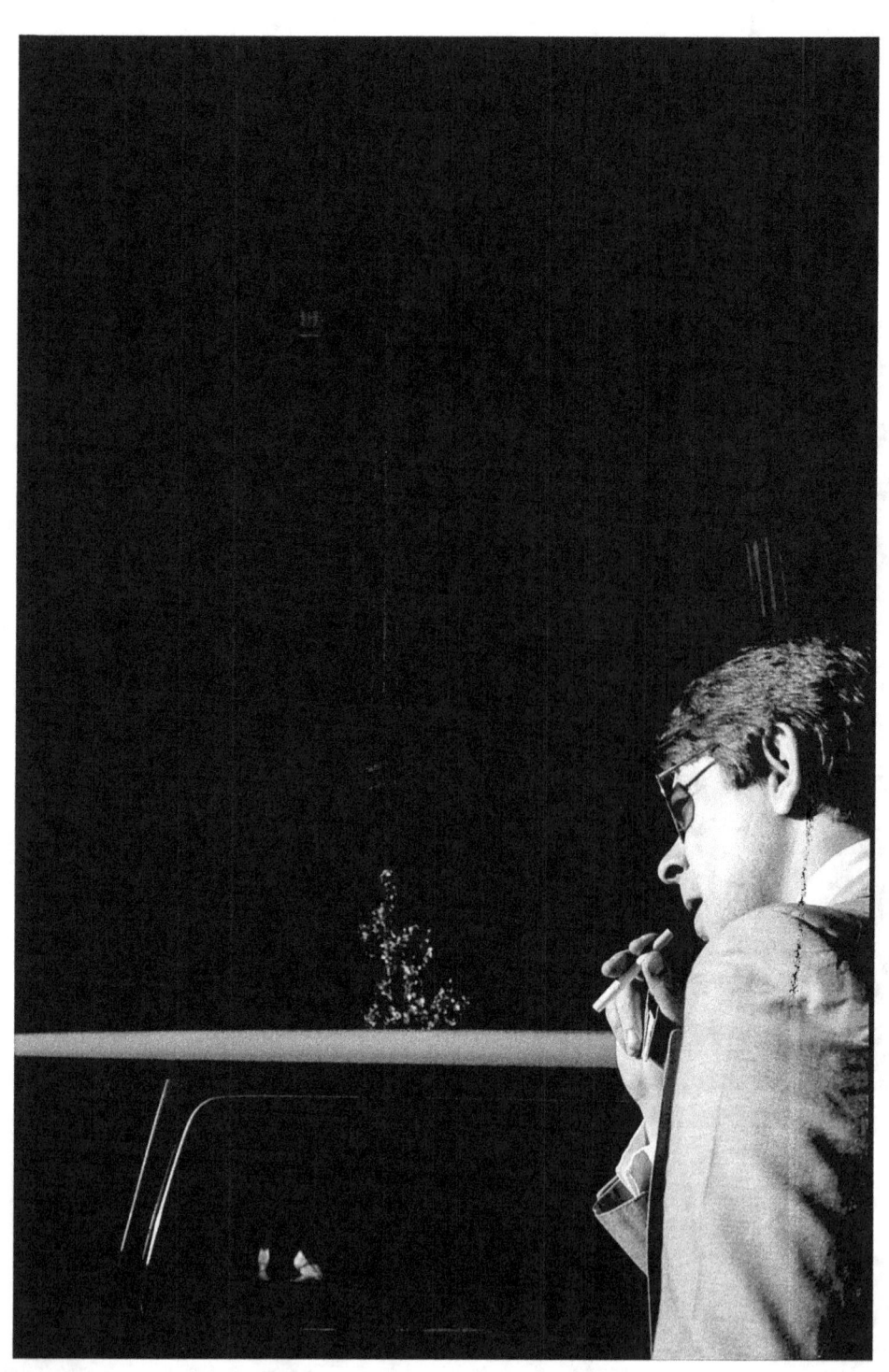

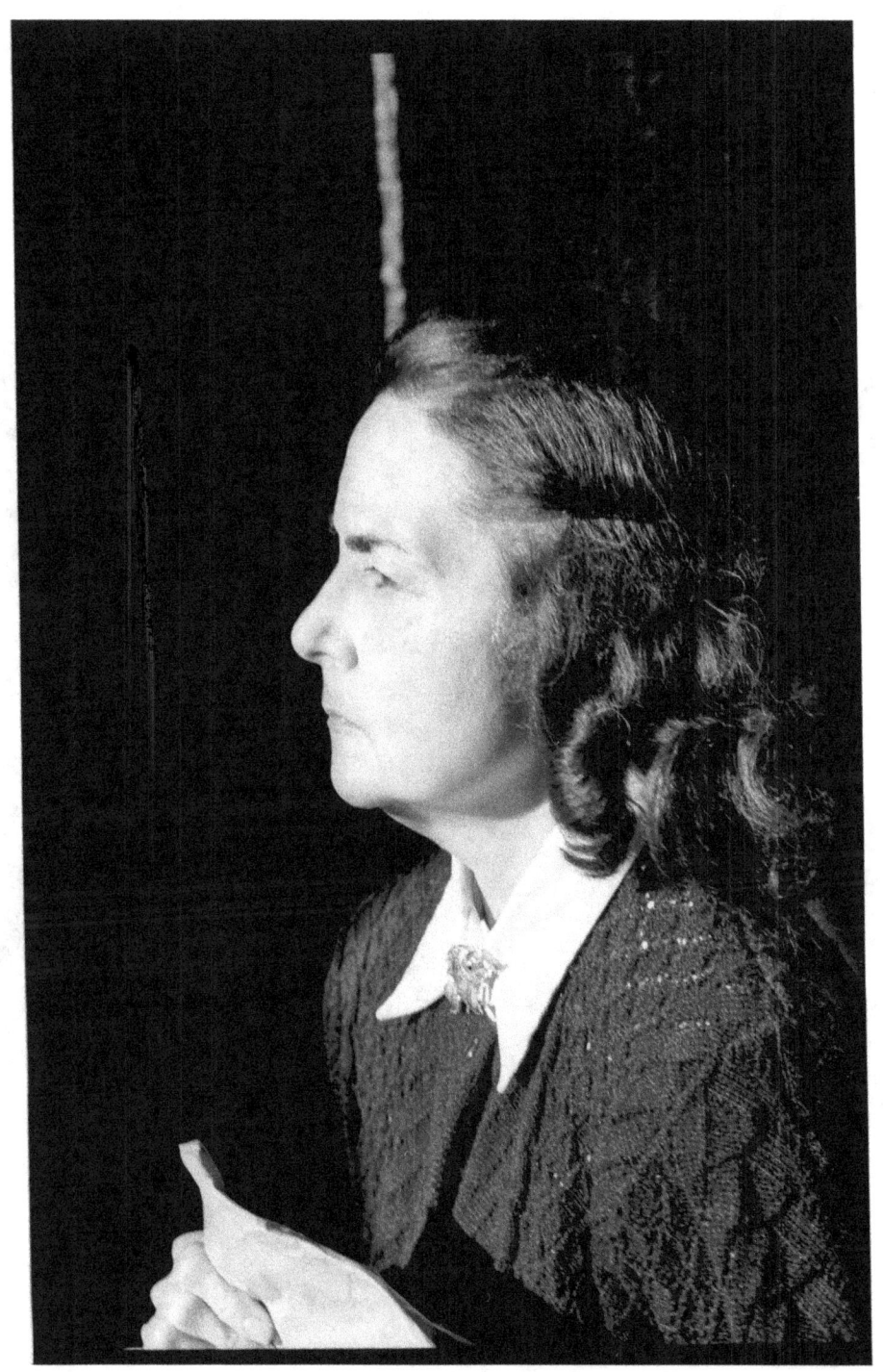

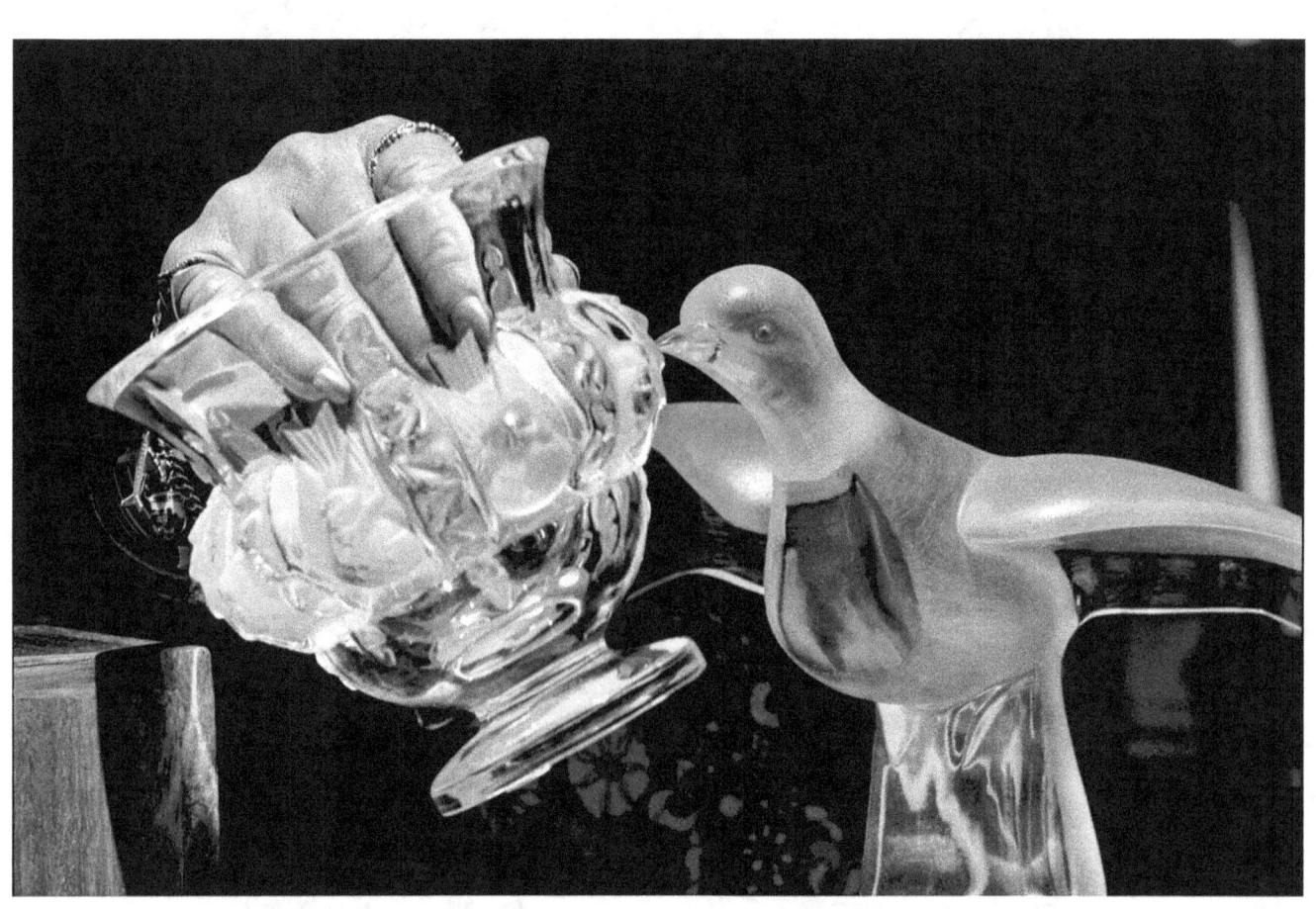

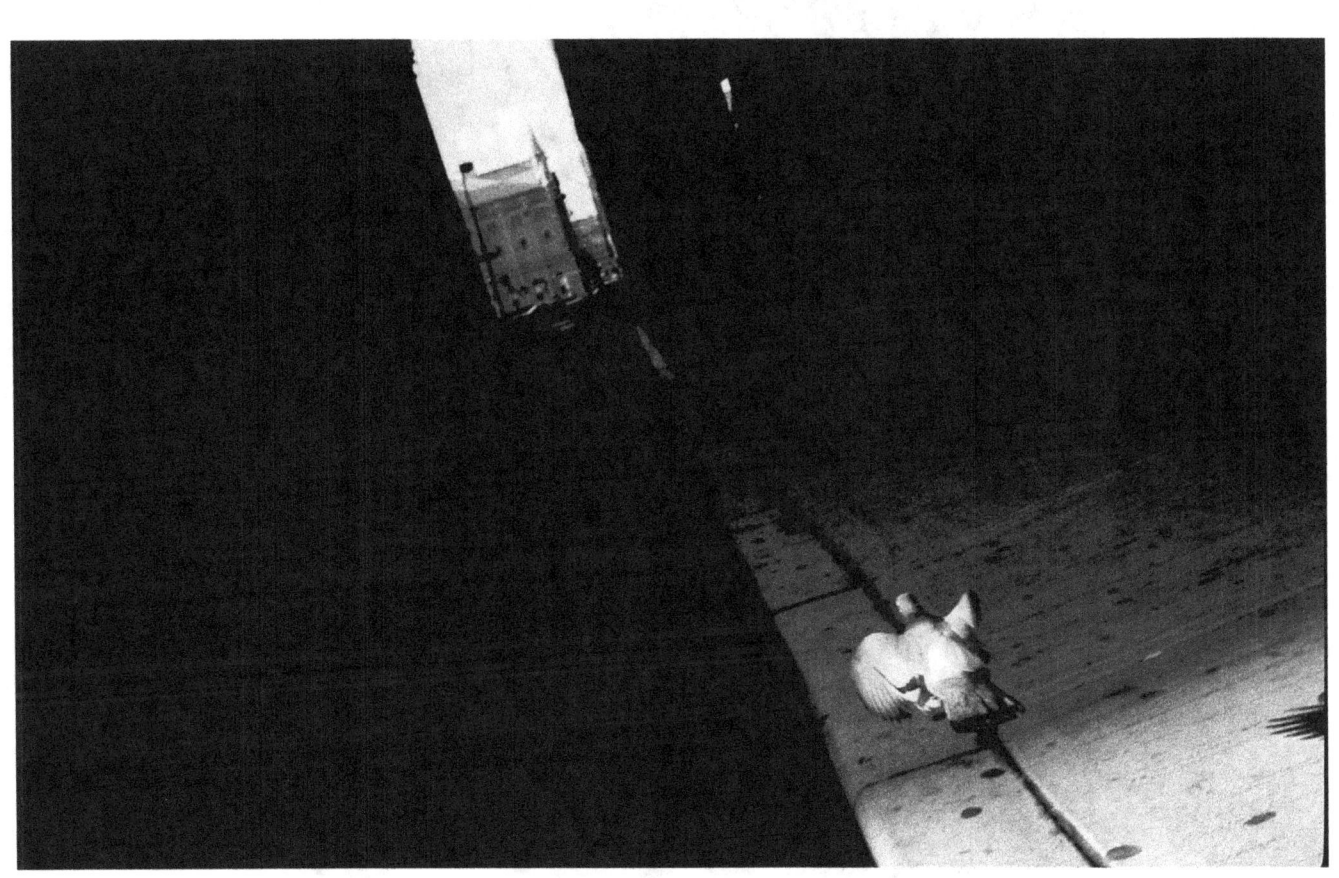

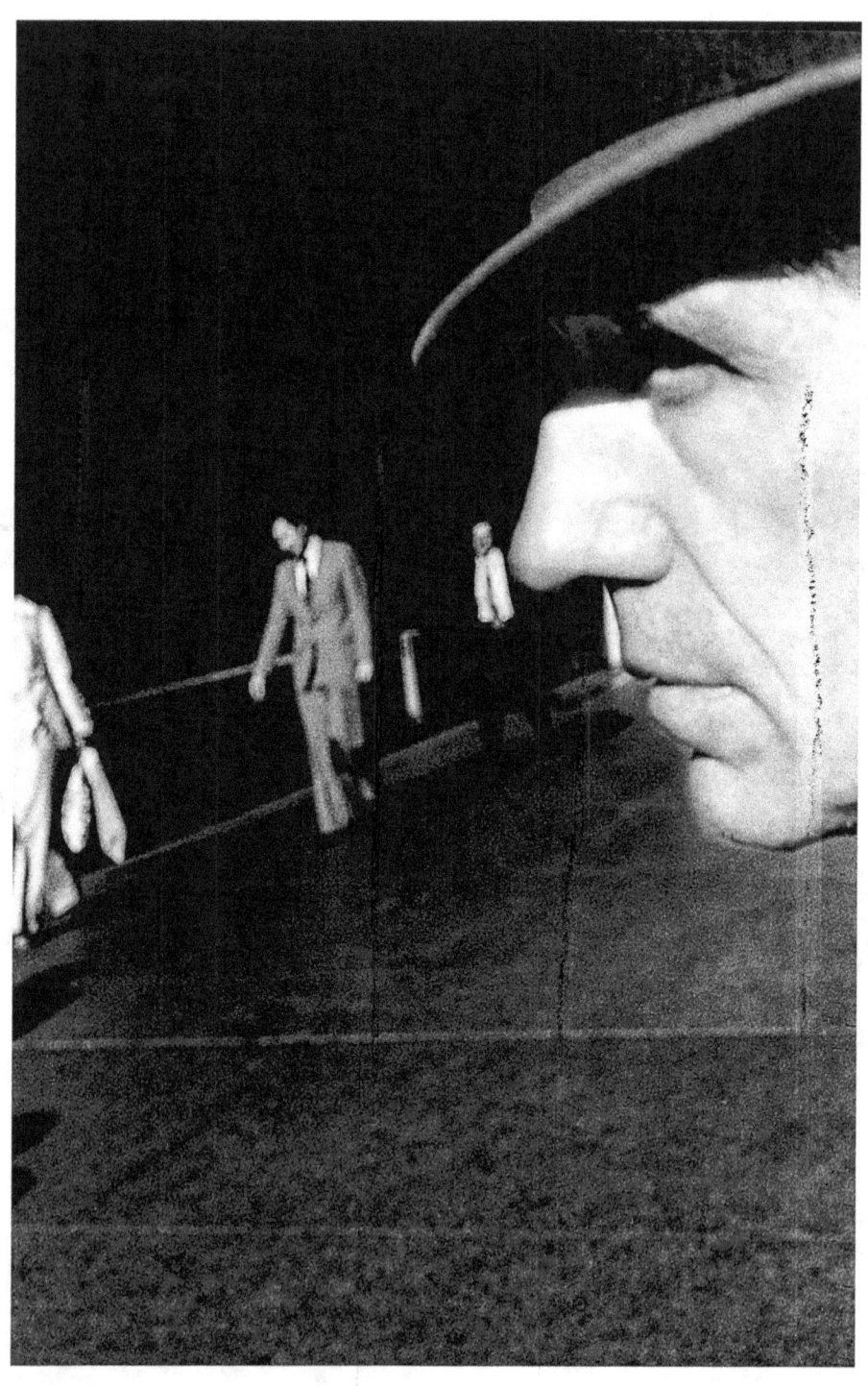

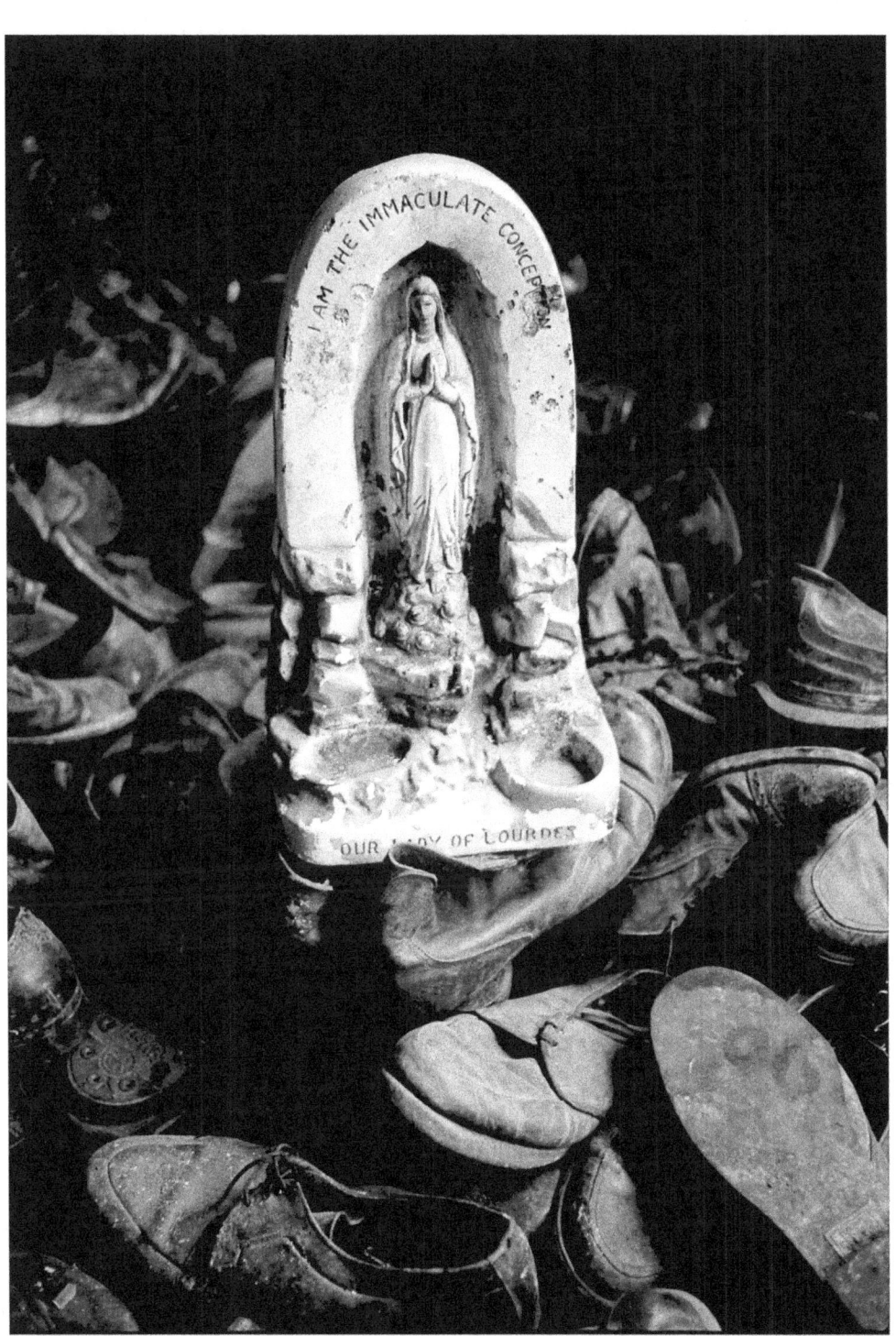